To Virginia and Rich,   4/11/14

THE
WORD CIRCUS

A LETTER-PERFECT BOOK

by
Richard Lederer

Illustrations by Dave Morice

Merriam-Webster, Incorporated
Springfield, Massachusetts

A GENUINE MERRIAM-WEBSTER

The name *Webster* alone is no guarantee of excellence. It is used by a number of publishers and may serve mainly to mislead an unwary buyer.

Merriam-Webster™ is the name you should look for when you consider the purchase of dictionaries or other fine reference books. It carries the reputation of a company that has been publishing since 1831 and is your assurance of quality and authority.

Copyright © 1998 Richard Lederer

Library of Congress Cataloging-in-Publication Data

Lederer, Richard.
    The word circus : a letter-perfect book / by Richard Lederer ; illustrations by David Morice.
        p.   cm.
    Includes bibliographical references (p.   ).
    ISBN 0-87779-354-9 (hardcover : alk. paper)
    1. English language—Lexicology—Problems, exercises, etc.
2. Word games. I. Title.
PE1574.L374 1998
423'.028—DC21   98-27000
                                                                  CIP

Printed and bound in the United States of America
234567IB009998
Designed by Steven Kapusta

To Ross and Faith Eckler,
for teaching the world
the ways of words
and making the alphabet dance

CONTENTS

THE BARKER

Once upon a time, when the sky was made of
canvas and the ground was made of sawdust,
elephants in tutus danced on their toes and
cradled showgirls in their trunks.

Once upon a time, fountains of red hair spouted from high white foreheads, and saggy, baggy
clowns spilled into our laughter.

Once upon a time, when we were young and
full of wonder, acrobats in spangled tights flew
through the air like birds, and plumed horses
pranced to the music of steam calliopes.

Once upon a time, there was magic in our
land, and that magic was the circus.

Ladies and gentlemen and children of all ages!
Hurry! Hurry! Hurry!
Step right up and into a ring-a-ding circus of words!
Inside you'll ooh and aah at tremendous, stupendous, end-over-endous
    words swinging from tent-tops!

words teetering on tightropes!

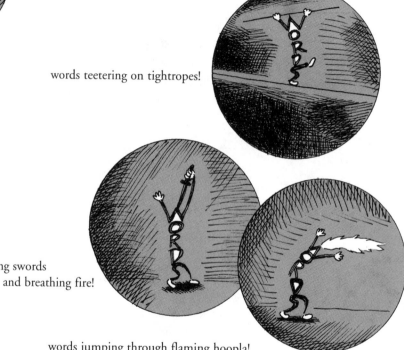

words swallowing swords
    and breathing fire!

words jumping through flaming hoopla!
words leaping onto the backs of galloping coursers!
(all the while maintaining their equine-imity!)
words thrusting their heads into the jaws of lions!
bestial words — from Noah's aardvark to on beyond zebra!
high-caliber words shot out of the canon of letter fun!

You'll laugh at

words somersaulting, heels over head!
words sporting, cavorting in billowy, pillowy clown suits!

words pedaling their unisyllables!

words perched high on stilts! midget words!

elephantine words! toy poodle words!

sideshow words with shapes beyond the arena of ordinary life!
words going for the juggler!

From alpha to omega,
    You can bet the alphabet,
Like a painting done by Degas,
    Will leap and pirouette.

See dancing words, entrancing words,
    Sterling words unfurling.
Watch prancing words, enhancing words,
    Whirling, twirling, swirling.

Honored patrons and matrons, now is the time to face the fact that you've been playing with letters for almost your whole lives. You've enjoyed juggling and snuggling letters in word searches, crossword puzzles, Scrabble, and jumble word challenges. Unless you've been a hermit, or, if you're a guy, a hismit, you have probably heard the likes of:

*The difference between a *champ* and a *chump* is *u*.

*The dictionary is the only place where success comes before work.

*What word becomes shorter when you add two letters to it?
Short.

*From what can you take the whole and still have some left over?
Wholesome.

*Why is the letter D like a naughty child?
Because it makes *ma mad*.

*Why is *noon* like the letter A?
Because it is in the middle of *day*.

*What starts with T, ends with T, and is full of T?
A *teapot*.

*Which letters are like a Roman emperor?
N and *P* because they are near *O*.

*What other letters are like a Roman emperor?
The *C*'s are.

*It occurs once in every minute, twice in every moment, and yet never in one hundred thousand years. What is it?
The letter *m*.

*A pastor put up a sign that read THIS IS A CH—CH. WHAT IS MISSING?
The answer is UR.

and

Smiles is the longest word in the English language because there's a *mile* between its first and last letters.

Your smile will indeed be a mile wide when you come to see that words stand ready to wreathe your face with grins, to soften the wrinkles of sorrow and the frowns of unalloyed reality.

Words are objects of art. Words are entertainment. Words are a circus, where all the humor is guaranteed to be in tents.

Come one! Come all! The Word Circus is in town. Hurry! Hurry! Scurry! Here you'll discover fun for the whole family — words you read and write and hear and speak each day. For the most part, the performers will be non-technical words and uncapitalized words — words that you live with every hour of your waking day. The Collide-O-Scope of Letters is the most democratic of all entertainments, available to everybody in all walks of life.

So run! Don't walk! You've already paid for your ticket to the bar-none Barnum and Ballyhoo letter-perfect circus, the colossus of all amusements, the Palace in Wonderland that runs Ringlings around all the others. Now take your seat in the biggest top of all, the sawdust stage of words.

The show now starts.
The letter play's the thing
Wherein we'll catch your
consciousness and sing!

THE BANDWAGON

Ladies and gentlemen!
Boys and girls! Noteworthy music lovers of all ages!
Now that you've paid the piper, I'm going to orchestrate an overture that will be music to your ears.

I also strive to strike a responsive chord. I don't want to chime in on your enjoyment and harp on the fact that I'm feeling fit as a fiddle, without playing second fiddle to anyone. I don't want to blow my own horn, but I do know my brass from my oboe. We at the Word Circus would never play it by ear or give you a song and dance with a second-string performance. I'm not going to soft-pedal any praise for our lyrical, harmonious English language. Rather, I'm going to pull out all the stops and drum up support for our melodic, mellifluous words. And that's not just whistling Dixie.

So let's hop on the bandwagon and face the music!

Now the tent grows dark, and the crowd grows hush.
  Then the spotlight shines, and the space grows lush
With the cymbals' clash and the tinkled heat,
  The triangle's ting and the snare drum's beat,
As our hungry hearts and the empty air
  Fill to the brim with a brassy blare.

Our jaws a-droop and our eyes a-light
  And our cheeks ablaze at the gorgeous sight:
All golden and crimson and purple and blue —
  A calliope dream that we never knew:
With the chest-deep pulse of the kettle drums,
  Into the ring the bandwagon comes.

Then the wha-wha-wha of the slide trombone,
  And the pitter-boink-boink of the xylophone,
And the umpa umpa umpa umps
  Of tubas kissed by men with mumps,
And the twang and the wang and the whacka whacka whack
  Of banjo wheels on a circus track.

Ah, the rattle and rhyme of the music's time
Brim our hungry hearts with a song sublime!

Ladies and gentlemen! As I crack my whip, the canvas castle fills with life. Onto the sawdust stage high steps our spectacular English language, the most tintinnabulating of the world's tongues.

Writer Michael Arlen once said, "English is the great Wurlitzer of language, the most perfect all-purpose instrument ever invented." With the world's most gargantuan vocabulary (more than three times as many words as German, in second place, more than four times as many as Russian, in third place, and more than six times as many as French, in fourth), English sings a different tune because it is the most magical, musical language in the world.

Let's start out with letter-perfect words.

Grammagrams are RT words that, when they are pronounced, consist entirely of letter sounds. Words such as *emcee, deejay,* and *veejay* that are actually formed from letter sounds are initialisms, not grammagrams. Listen now to the FX of the most popular two-syllable grammagrammatical attractions:

any (NE)
beady (BD)
cagey (KG)
cutey (QT)
decay (DK)
easy (EZ)
empty (MT)
envy (NV)

essay (SA)
excel (XL)
excess (XS)
icy (IC)
ivy (IV)
kewpie (QP)
seedy (CD)
tepee (TP)

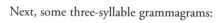

Next, some three-syllable grammagrams:

devious (DVS)   enemy (NME)   escapee (SKP)   opium (OPM)
effendi (FND)   envious (NVS)   odious (ODS)   tedious (TDS)

Now four syllables:

anemone (NMNE)   arcadian (RKDN)   excellency (XLNC)

And the longest grammagrams are — ta da! — the pentasyllabic *expediency* (XPDNC) and *obediency* (OBDNC)!

Letter artists have come up with a number of variations beyond the grammagrammatical sounding out of individual words. Lewis Carroll, author of *Alice's Adventures in Wonderland* and other fantasies, played upon the sounds of letters in composing a letter to Annie Rodgers:

> My dear Annie,
>   I send you
> A picture, which I hope will
> B one that you will like to
> C. If your Mamma should
> D sire one like it, I could
> E sily get her one.

A classic dialogue is this string of letters that don't exactly match but that approximate words. The scene is a restaurant, and the characters are a breakfast diner and a server:

> Diner (to server): F U N E X?
> Server: Y S V F X.
> Diner: F U N E M?
> Server: Y S V F M.
> Diner: O K L F M N X.

Now hear the music of some letter-perfect verse. Keep in mind that the same letter twice in a row sounds like a plural. For example, *II* means "eyes."

	Translation
YURYY	Why you are wise
Is EZ to C	Is easy to see.
U should B called	You should be called
"XLNC."	"Excellency."
U XEd NE	You exceed any
MT TT.	Empty tease.
I NV how U	I envy how you
XL with EE.	Excel with ease.

Here's an almost century-old example of letter play, by H. C. Dodge, that appeared in the July 1903 *Woman's Home Companion*. ICQ out so that I can CU have fun translating the sound FX of this poem:

The farmer leads no EZ life.
    The CD sows will rot;
And when at EV rests from strife,
    His bones will AK lot.

In DD has to struggle hard
    To EK living out;
If IC frosts do not retard
    His crops, there'll BA drought.

The hired LP has to pay
    Are awful AZ, too;
They CK rest when he's away,
    Nor NE work will do.

Both NZ cannot make to meet,
    And then for AD takes
Some boarders, who so RT eat,
    And E no money makes.

Of little UC finds his life;
    Sick in old AG lies;
The debts he OZ leaves his wife,
    And then in PC dies.

To close our overture of letter music, we present one of the most astonishing puzzles of all time. Fill in the four-by-four puzzle square below:

1	2	3	4
2			
3			
4			

<table>
<tr><td>Across</td><td>Down</td></tr>
</table>

Across
1. What mosquitoes do.
2. What snakes do.
3. What dogs do
4. What teeth do

Down
1. Insects
2. Optical organs
3. Annoy
4. Comfort

Here is the resulting grid:

1 B	2 I	3 T	4 E
2 B	I	T	E
3 B	I	T	E
4 B	I	T	E

The Down rows now read 1. *bees* (B's) 2. *eyes* (I's) 3. *tease* (T's) 4. *ease* (E's).

One of the oral and aural delights of our English language is its uncommon stockpile of homophones — words — such as *oral* and *aural* — that are pronounced alike but are spelled differently and with different meanings:

No humor,
No happiness.
Know humor;
Know happiness.

Hear here. Let's start with twenty words that become their own homophones when their first letter is beheaded:

aisle/isle	knew/new	llama/lama	wrest/rest
hour/our	knickers/nickers	Psalter/salter	wretch/retch
knap/nap	knight/night	scent/cent	wright/right
knave/nave	knit/nit	whole/hole	write/rite
kneed/need	knot/not	wrap/rap	wrote/rote

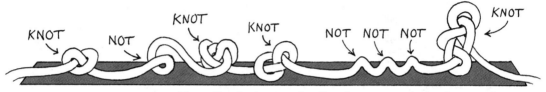

Now take a look at another list of twenty words that become their own homophones when their last letter is curtailed:

add/ad	butt/but	flue/flu	ore/or
bee/be	bye/by	fore/for	please/pleas
belle/bell	canvass/canvas	inn/in	sow/so
block/bloc	caste/cast	lamb/lam	too/to
borne/born	damn/dam	lapse/laps	wee/we

Next up, twenty pairs of words that are homophonic when we delete an internal letter:

aunt/ant	choral/coral	maize/maze	overrate/overate
boarder/border	fined/find	mined/mind	reign/rein
boulder/bolder	guild/gild	mooed/mood	seamen/semen
callous/callus	hoarse/horse	mourning/morning	two/to
cannon/canon	lead/led	oar/or	waive/wave

Now for the most extraordinary of all homophone acts — twenty high-stepping homophonic pairs that turn out to be anagrams of each other!:

bear/bare	hide/hied	pride/pried	steak/stake
break/brake	hose/hoes	reed/rede	tale/tael
discrete/discreet	meet/mete	rude/rued	tear/tare
gale/Gael	ore/o'er	ruse/rues	tide/tied
great/grate	pear/pare	seer/sere	wear/ware

What do you call a naked grizzly? A *bare bear*. What do you call an equine with a sore throat? A *hoarse horse*. Ladies and gentlemen, around the sawdust circle troops a troupe consisting of a *dear deer*, a *grisly grizzly*, a *new gnu*, a *foul fowl*, a *towed toad*, an *ant aunt*, a *gorilla guerrilla* (note all five major vowels in that pair), a *llama lama*, a *mousse moose*, a *dough doe*, and a *roe row*. Notice the *hare hair*, the *mussel muscle*, the *hart heart*, the *lynx links*, the *lox locks*, the *oriole aureole*, and the *mite might*. At the tail end of the parade, watch a *boar bore*, a *burro burrow*, a *mule mewl*, a *bee be*, a *whale wail*, a *flea flee*, *ewes use*, and *does doze*.

An anonymous poem written more than a century ago opens:

> A pretty deer is dear to me,
>   A hare with downy hair;
>   love a hart with all my heart,
>   But barely bear a bear.

These zoological matches are among the thousands of homophonic pairs in our language, but what about triples and quadruples?

The greatest aerialist of all time was a Mexican, Alfredo Cordona. In 1930, after years of practice, Cordona achieved what to the whole circus world had been an impossibility — no less than a triple somersault! It is estimated that, to achieve that feat, he flew through the air at sixty miles per hour.

Now gaze upward at the canvas sky and watch words whirl through their triple somersaults. Have you heard about the successful perfume manufacturer? His business made a lot of sense (scents, cents). That's one triple. Here are sixty-eight more!

Excluded are foreign words, regional pronunciations, proper nouns, and arcane and archaic words. Musical notes (*do, re, mi*), and letters of the alphabet are allowed (we'll say aloud), since they are listed in most dictionaries:

adds/ads/adze
aisle/I'll/isle
aye/eye/I
b/be/bee
bald/balled/bawled
beau/bo/bow
bole/boll/bowl
born/borne/bourn
brr/bur/burr
burro/borough/burrow
bused/bussed/bust
c/sea/see
cay/k/quay
cent/scent/sent
chord/cord/cored
cite/sight/site
clamber/clammer/clamor
cue/q/queue
dew/do/due

do (in music)/doe/dough
does (deer)/doughs/doze
firs/furs/furze
flew/flu/flue
for/fore/four
frees/freeze/frieze
gild/gilled/guild
gnu/knew/new
heal/heel/he'll
hi/hie/high
hoard/horde/whored
holey/holy/wholly
idle/idol/idyll
knead/kneed/need
knows/no's/nose
load/lode/lowed
lochs/locks/lox
meat/meet/mete
nay/nee/neigh

o/oh/owe
p/pea/pee
palate/pallet/palette
pare/pair/pear
peak/peek/pique
poor/pore/pour
praise/prays/preys
rain/reign/rein
raise/rays/raze
raiser/razer/razor
rapped/rapt/wrapped
read/rede/reed
road/rode/rowed
rood/rude/rued
roomie/roomy/rheumy
sear/seer/sere
sol/sole/soul
sold/soled/souled
their/there/they're

DO RE MI FA **SOL** LA TI DO

to/too/two
toad/toed/towed
vane/vain/vein
vial/viol/vile

wail/wale/whale
ware/wear/where
way/weigh/whey

we/wee/whee!
weal/we'll/wheel
whined/wind/wined
y's/wise/whys

And now, ladies and gentlemen, lift your eyes once again for a company of — not double, not triple, but — *quadruple* homophones!:

air/ere/err/heir
bi/buy/by/bye
carat/caret/carrot/karat
c's/seas/sees/seize

ewe/u/yew/you
ewes/u's/use/yews
oar/o'er/or/ore
p's/peas/pease/pees

right/rite/wright/write
sew/so/sol/sow
t/tea/tee/ti
t's/teas/tease/tees

You'll note that the homophones in a select few of these clusters begin with three different letters:

air/ere/err/heir
aye/eye/I
ewe/u/yew/you
ewes/u's/use/yews
gnu/knew/new

Raise and *raze*, *raiser* and *razer*, and *petalous* and *petalless* happen to be three homophonic pairs of opposite meaning. *Oral* and *aural* may also qualify.

Write/rite/wright/right form a double beheadment; decapitating the initial *w* produces two different homophones!

YEW AND EYE!

Now we're going to call you on the homophone one last time.

Hears a rye peace eye maid up inn my idol thyme. Aye rote it four yew two sea Howe homophones Cannes seam sew whiled from there knows write too they're tows. With pried, eye no it will knot boar ewe. Its meant two bee red allowed:

A Bazaar Tail

One *night* a *knight* on a *hoarse horse*
   Rode out upon a *road*.
This *male wore mail* for *war* and *would*
   Explore a *wood* that glowed.

His *tale* I'll tell from head to *tail*.
   I'll *write* his *rite* up *right*.
A hidden *site* our hero found,
   A *sight* that I shall *cite*.

With *woe* he shouted, *"Whoa!"* as *rain*
   Without a *break* did *reign*.
To *brake*, he pulled the *rein*, and like
   A shattered *pane*, felt *pain*.

The *poor* knight met a *witch, which* made
   Sweat *pour* from every *pore*.
He'd never *seen* a *scene* like that.
   His *sore* heart couldn't *soar*.

Then they a game for truffles played,
   In which he *mined* her *mind*.
To prove who was the *better bettor*
   And *find* who should be *fined*.

He *won one* twice, he *won two, too*.
   To *grate* on her felt *great*.
To *wrest* the *rest*, he went *for four*,
   And, at the *fore, ate eight*.

Due to her loss, the *mourning* witch,
   'Midst *morning mist* and *dew,*
Her truffles *missed.* I *know no way,*
   Do I, to *weigh* her rue.

Our knight began to *reel,* for *real.*
   The *world whirled,* so to speak.
All the *days* of the *week* his *sole soul* felt
   The dizzy *daze* of the *weak.*

Our *heir* to knighthood gave it up.
   He felt the *fare* not *fair.*
His *wholly holy sword soared* up
   As he *threw* it *through* the *air.*

The bell has *tolled,* I'm *told.* The *hour*
   To end *our* tale draws nigh.
Without *ado,* I bid *adieu,*
   So *by* your leave, *bye-bye.*

Homophones demonstrate how many different letters or letter combinations can produce the same sound. If you need more proof, gaze upon a twenty-two word sentence in which every word contains a long oh sound, yet each of those sounds is spelled differently→

Let's now reverse our field. Not only can single sounds be represented by many different letters, but certain letters can repre-

ALTHOUGH YEOMEN FOLK OWE PHARAOH'S VAUD BUREAU'S DEPOT HOED OATS, CHAUVINISTIC VAN GOGH, SWALLOWING COGNAC OH SO SOULFULLY, SEWS GROSSGRAIN, PICOTED, BROOCHED CHAPEAUX!?

sent a wide variety of sounds. The *e*'s in *reentered,* for example, have four different pronunciations, including one silence. Note watt happens to the sound of the *c* when the base word *electric* becomes *electricity* and *electrician.* "Ohm my. Wire you ready to socket to me? This is absolutely shocking and re-volting," you incandesce. "I re-fuse to believe this!"

The letter string *ough* is the most protean of all, sounded at least ten different ways:

bough	cough	hiccough	rough	through
bought	dough	lough	thoroughbred	trough

To illustrate how tough *ough* can be (and accepting both *trawf* and *trawth* as legitimate soundings of *trough*), we'll insert one or two or three letters at a time after the *t* in *tough* to create:

tough	trough	though	through	thorough,

none of which rhyme with each other.

Tough Stough
The wind was rough.
The cold was grough.
She kept her hands
Inside her mough.

And even though
She loved the snough,
The weather was
A heartless fough.

It chilled her through.
Her lips turned blough.
The frigid flakes
They blough and flough.

They shook each bough,
And she saw hough
The animals froze —
Each cough and sough.

While at their trough,
Just drinking brough,
Were frozen fast
Each slough and mough.

It made her hiccough —
Worse than a sticcough.
She drank hot cocoa
For an instant piccough.

Going from bard to verse, here's another poem. As you read the ditty, note the unusual pattern of end-rhymes:

A Heteronymble Poem

Ladies and gentlemen! Toward me *bow.*
Please watch the show; don't draw the *bow.*
Please don't try to start a *row.*
Sit peacefully, all in a *row.*
Don't squeal like a big, fat *sow.*
Do not the seeds of discord *sow.*

In the first, third, and fifth lines of this poem, *bow, row,* and *sow* all rhyme with *cow* and mean, respectively, "to bend," "argument," and "female pig." In the second, fourth, and sixth lines, *bow, row,* and *sow* all rhyme with *low* and mean, respectively, "a weapon," "a line," and "to plant."

Bow, row, and *sow* are choice examples of heteronyms — words with the same spelling as other words but with different pronunciations and meanings. While homophones change letters to produce the same sound, heteronyms retain their letters to produce different sounds. Hence this heteronymic riddle ↑

Membership in the exclusive club of heteronyms is strict, and tandems such as *resume* and *resumé* and *pate* and *pâté* are not admitted because the accent constitutes a change in spelling. Pseudo-heteronymic pairs such as *insult* (noun) and *insult* (verb), *refuse* (noun) and *refuse* (verb), *read* (present-tense verb) and *read* (past-tense verb), and *primer* (beginner's book) and *primer* (base coat of paint) are fairly common in the English language, but they are not true heteronyms because their etymologies are so closely related.

Here's a Word Circus list of genuine, authentic, certified heteronyms. Accept no substitutes:

agape	bow	converse	dove
alum	buffet	coop	drawer
axes	coax	deserts	entrance
bases	console	do	evening
bass	content	does	fillet

grave	number	reside	sol
hinder	object	resign	sow
incense	overage	resort	stingy
lead	palled	route	sundries
liver	palling	row	supply
lower	palsy	rugged	tarry
lunged	pasty	sake	taxes
mare	peaked	salve	tear
minute	present	secretive	toots
mobile	pussy	sewer	tower
mole	putting	shower	tush
moped	rape	singer	unionized
more	raven	skied	wicked
multiply	reprobate	slaver	wind
nestling	resent	slough	wound

Three words in this array are plurals of two different singulars. *Axes* is the plural of both *axe* and *axis, bases* is the plural of both *base* and *basis,* and *taxes* is the plural of both *tax* and *taxis* (the response of a simple organism to a stimulus). The pronunciation of *axes, bases,* and *taxes* depends on which singular is the axis and basis.

Many a fan of the Word Circus has heard a sentence that can be spoken but not written: "There are three ways to spell *(to, too, two)*." Here's a sentence that can be written but not spoken: "There are three ways to pronounce *slough*." If we are talking about a place of deep mud or mire, we say "sloo"; about a backwater, "slou"; about the action of casting off, as the skin of a snake, "sluff." Hence, *slough* is the only triple heteronym in English.

True heteronymic pairs that are not clearly related in word formation are among the rarest of occurrences. That's why the heteronymble parade in the Word Circus consists only of a *bass bass,* a *nestling nestling,* a *pussy pussy,* and a *mole mole. Does* the presence of *does* add to the parade? Did you watch as a *dove dove?* Would you like to see a *sow sow* and a *raven raven?* As you read the poem on page 20 aloud, you'll be astonished at what happens to the pronunciations and meanings of each twosome:

A Hymn to Heteronyms

Please go through the *entrance* of our circus show.
  We guarantee it will *entrance* you.
The *content* will certainly make you *content*,
  And the knowledge gained sure will enhance you.

A clown *moped* around when the circus refused
  For him a new *moped* to buy.
The *incense* he burned did *incense* him to go
  On a *tear* with a *tear* in his eye.

He *ragged* on his bosses, felt they ran him *ragged*.
  Their just *deserts* they never got.
He imagined them lost in *deserts* quite vast,
  So sandy, so arid, so hot.

A *number* of times he felt *number*, all *wound*
  Up, like one with a *wound*, not a wand.
His new TV *console* just couldn't *console*
  Or *slough* off a *slough* of despond.

The *rugged* clown paced 'round his shaggy *rugged* room,
  All *evening* his clothes he did rend,
Evening out the cross-*winds* of his ire,
  As our circus act *winds* to its end.

At *present*, our clown will *present* you a show;
  So your *liver* will feel *liver* after.
A good circus clown's always in short *supply*.
  He can *supply* draw out our laughter.

Apostrophes are strange symbols. They don't mean anything until they're put between the letters of a word in a contraction, and then they mean that something has been taken out. In addition, an apostrophe often transmutes the pronunciation of one word into another:

An Apostrophe to Love
When she said *we'd*
Be shortly *wed,*
Her dad said, *"He'll*
Be damned to *hell."*

She asked if *I'd*
Obeyed my *id.*
I asked if *she'll*
Remove her *shell.*

If only *she'd*
Come to my *shed!*
Together *we'll*
Be feeling *well.*

But if I *can't*
Believe her *cant,*
I guess that *I'll*
Be feeling *ill.*

I'm sure that *we're*
What once we *were,*
But if we *won't,*
It is our *wont.*

That punctual little poem capitalizes on a mark of punctuation. Other words capitalize on capitalization.

A capitonym is a word that changes pronunciation and meaning when it is capitalized. Take the world of tennis. We can muster Austrian star Thomas Muster, pronounced "Mooster." Would you like a date with Japanese champ Kimiko Date ("Dahtay")? Hey, guy. Don't forget French tennis luminary Guy Forget, pronounced "Gee Forjay," a double capitonym.

Joining Muster, Forget, and Date are Bill Amend, who draws the comic strip *Fox Trot*, and Berkeley Breathed, creator of *Bloom County* and *Outland*.

Now sound out this list of prominent capitonyms in both their lowercase and capitalized forms:

amend	colon	guy	messier	polish
askew	concord	herb	millet	rainier
august	date	job	muster	ravel
begin	degas	levy	natal	reading
breathed	forget	lima	nice	tangier

Job's Job
In *August,* an *august* patriarch,
Was *reading* an ad in *Reading,* Mass.
Long-suffering *Job* secured a *job*
To *polish* piles of *Polish* brass.

Herb's Herbs
An *herb* store owner, name of *Herb,*
Moved to *rainier* Mt. *Rainier,*
It would have been so *nice* in *Nice,*
And even *tangier* in *Tangier.*

Now that you have listened to the music of letters at play, let's close with the sounds of silence. All twenty-six letters in our alphabet are mute in one or another word. Here's a lineup of such contexts to demonstrate the deafening silence that rings through English orthography:

A: bread, marriage, pharaoh
B: doubt, subtle, thumb
C: blackguard, indict, yacht
D: edge, handkerchief, Wednesday
E: fore, height, yeoman
F: halfpenny
G: gnarl, reign, tight
H: ghost, heir, yacht
I: business, seize, Sioux
J: marijuana, rijstaffel
K: blackguard, knob, sackcloth
L: half, salmon, would
M: mnemonic

N: column, damn, hymn
O: country, laboratory, tortoise
P: cupboard, psychology, receipt
Q: lacquer, racquet
R: chevalier, forecastle, Worcester
S: debris, island, rendezvous
T: gourmet, listen, tsar
U: circuit, dough, intrigue
V: fivepence
W: answer, cockswain, wrist
X: faux pas, grand prix, Sioux
Y: aye, crayon
Z: pince-nez, rendezvous

Now consider the opposite phenomenon, words in which a letter is sounded even though that letter is not spelled. In *Xerox,* for example, the letter *z* speaks even though it does not appear in the base word. Here's a complete alphabet of silent hosts:

Y: WINE

A: eight
B: W-shaped
C: sea
D: Taoism
E: happy
F: tough
G: jeer
H: nature
I: eye
J: margarine
K: quiche
L: W-shaped
M: grandpa

N: comptroller
O: bureau
P: hiccough
Q: cue
R: colonel
S: civil
T: missed
U: ewe
V: of
W: one
X: decks
Y: wine
Z: xylophone

William Congreve penned the famous (but oft misquoted) pronouncement "Music hath charms to soothe a savage breast." Letter play hath charms to soothe a word lover's breast and mind. William Shakespeare began his comedy *Twelfth Night* with the line:

Play on we shall.

ANAGRAM THE JUGGLER

Ladies and gentlemen, welcome to the unparalleled, incomparable, sensational Word Circus, the Greatest Show on Earth. Watch words come out of the wordwork. Laugh at our lexcellent tour de farces! Gasp as letters fly through the air with the greatest of *E*'s. Thrill as you become The Wizard of Ahs or A Lass in Wonderland!

Can you create one word out of the letters in *new door*?

The answer is (ha ha) *one word*. The letters in *new door* are the same as those in *one word*, except in a different order.

When is enough not enough?

When you rearrange the letters in *enough,* you get *one hug.* Everybody knows that one hug is never enough!

A very early puzzle of this type appeared in the July 16, 1796, issue of *Weekly Museum,* under the name "Matilda":

An insect of the smallest kind
  If you transpose, you soon will find
That from all mortals I do quickly fly;
  When gone, my loss in vain they'll mourn.
In vain will wish for my return,
  Tho' now to kill me, ev'ry act they try.

The answer is *mite/time.*

These riddles all involve anagrams. An anagram is a rearrangement of all the letters in a familiar word, phrase, or name to form another word, phrase, or name. Feast your eyes on a parade of anagram crackers as onto the circus stage trot a *shore horse, a steed teased* and *seated,* a *smug tan mustang,* an *orchestra carthorse,* and a *point pinto on tip.* Are you ready to *greet* an *egret, count a toucan,* and recoil at a *snake sneak?:*

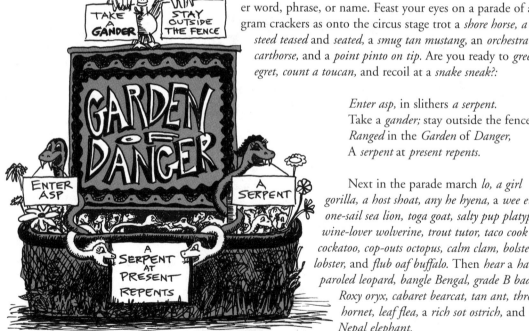

Enter asp, in slithers *a serpent.*
Take a *gander;* stay outside the fence:
Ranged in the *Garden* of *Danger,*
A *serpent* at *present repents.*

Next in the parade march *lo, a girl gorilla, a host shoat, any he hyena,* a *wee ewe, one-sail sea lion, toga goat, salty pup platypus, wine-lover wolverine, trout tutor, taco cook cockatoo, cop-outs octopus, calm clam, bolster lobster,* and *flub oaf buffalo.* Then *hear* a *hare, paroled leopard, bangle Bengal, grade B badger, Roxy oryx, cabaret bearcat, tan ant, throne hornet, leaf flea,* a *rich sot ostrich,* and *the Nepal elephant.*

And there's more! — *sobbing gibbons, snorted rodents, unshod hounds, snug gnus, spooled poodles, slow owls, Canarsie canaries, mescal camels, spider prides,* and *noiseless lionesses.* At *least,* we'll *steal stale tales* of *slate teals.* For fun we'll close with *ten skit kittens* in a *cat act.*

She can twirl balls, clubs, plates, hoops, or flaming torches, but she's best when she's spinning letters. She starts with three letters, and when she really gets them going, she adds another and another and another and another and another and another and another, until the audience bursts into applause.

ANA GRAM
ANAGRAMS
HERSELF

Ladies and Gentlemen! Boys and girls! Children of all ages! Don't *waddle!* Don't *dawdle!* It's time for Anagramarama! It's *tedious outside,* so stay inside and view the fun *residing* at *ringside.*

I give you a *genuine ingenue,* the high *priest* of *esprit* and *ripest sprite* of letter play of the highest *stripe.*

I *enlist* you to be *silent* and *listen* to the *inlets* of my *tinsel* words. As we *begin* our *binge* of letter juggling, *please* don't even think about falling *asleep,* or your *retina* will not *retain* the *overt trove* of *laudatory, adulatory* letter wizardry, which has for too long *continued unnoticed.*

Simple logic *impels* your positive *reactions* to Ana Gram's *creations.* Among *robust turbos,* she's an absolute *dynamo,* even on a *Monday* — a *gagster* who will *stagger* you with her *latent talent.* She's the *antagonist* of *stagnation,* the *flauntress* of *artfulness,* and the *patroness* of letter shuffling because she knows how to *transpose* a *sword* into *words,* which then *float aloft.* Each *emphatic, empathic seraph phrase,* each *snatch* of her *chants,* will *stanch* any trace of *mental lament* and *reclaim* the *miracle* of language.

For *various* reasons, Ana Gram is a *saviour* who *loves* to *solve* your woes and who *repeals* any *relapse.* Her *stagery gyrates* the *grayest* spirit. Before you *reunite* with your *retinue* or retreat through the *ingress,* please attend to this greatest of *singers,* a *singer* who *reigns* and will never *resign* as our *merriest rimester.* She's one of those crowd-*pleaser leapers* whose *dances ascend* to the *highest heights* as she performs a *toe dance* while relating an *anecdote.*

Ana Gram's *persistent prettiness* earns her *direct credit* for *regally* and *largely* curing any *allergy* in the *gallery.* No *dictionary* is *indicatory* of the *elation* you will experience down to your very *toenail,* a joy that will — from the *fringes* of your *fingers,* from your *elbow* to *below* the *bowel,* from your *bared beard* to your *viler liver* to your *venal navel,* from your *ears* to your *arse,* from the top of the *spine* to the tip of the *penis* — *roost* in the *roots* of your *torso.*

She is the very *heart* of the *earth,* a *damsel* who merits *medals.* With a *lovely volley* of letters,

HEART OF THE EARTH

she juggles a *cheap peach,* an *Argentine tangerine,* and *solemn lemons* and *melons.* At the same time she *reaps, pares,* and then manages to *spear pears* while twirling *pastel plates* (a *staple* of her act) and balancing a *maraschino* on her nose and playing two *harmonicas.*

Pleased by what has *elapsed* and astounded by such *climaxes,* everyone *exclaims* that it would be impossible to *reproduce* her *procedure* to *intoxicate* your *excitation.* She never *mutilates,* only will *stimulate ultimates.* She will not *enervate,* and you will *venerate.* She'll *edify* and you will *deify* the *luster* of the *result* she'll unfailingly *rustle* up.

Lucky ladies and gentlemen! *Cripes!* Just think of the *prices* we offer, as advertised in *English* on the *shingle* that adorns our booth:

> DISCOUNTER INTRODUCES REDUCTIONS

Look closely at the *poster,* and *presto! — boing! bingo! —* you'll see an *integral alerting, altering, relating triangle.* What we have here is a trianagram — three ten-letter words, each a rearrangement of the other two! Now I, your Word Circus pitchman, will be busy *mastering emigrants streaming* (a nine-letter trianagram) into the tent. I hope that someone will have *cautioned* them not to have *auctioned* off their *education* (yet another nine-letter trianagram).

I, a *magnate gateman* who *patrols* these *portals* with your kind *permission,* have the *impression* that you brand me a *blabbing, babbling funfair ruffian,* a *has-been banshee,* a *tearing ingrate, infield infidel,* and an *errant ranter.* You may wish to *compile* a *polemic lamenting* my *alignment* as one of those *nameless salesmen* and *dishonest hedonists* who are full of *tangible bleating* and *impressing simperings.* You may claim that I who *ratchet* up the *chatter* with *supersonic percussion* am a *rowdy, wordy vice-dean* of *deviance.* You will be *eager* to *agree* that I'm a *trifling, flirting baritone obtainer* of *untidy nudity* who *seldom models* his *ideals* for *ladies.*

I may *madden* you and cause you to *demand* that I be *damned,* before you *depart,* convinced that I have *prated* and should be hoist on my own *petard, bombed,* and *mobbed.* But any *unstirred intruders* and *outbred doubters* who may *obtrude* should come to the *realization* that people tend to *ratio-*

ANA GRAM
JUGGLES
HERSELF

nalize. Irately and *tearily,* I tell you that, in *reality,* to be *portrayed* as one so *predatory* causes me *mental lament.* Anyone who accuses me of being a *usurping, pursuing, daemonic comedian* is simply being an *inconsistent nonscientist.*

Truth be told, I'm an *Einstein* of the *nineties* — *a gentleman, an elegant man* who gets *blamed* because I have *ambled* into *bedlam.* It's one of the *noisier ironies. However, whoever* enters needs no *caveat* to *vacate* this *auction* with *caution.* I *certify* that I will *rectify* the situation and *deposit* the *dopiest rowdies* and *weirdos* in the *closest closets.*

The *charisma* of Ana's performance *is a charm,* a *charm* that you see *march* before your eyes. In her, you *observe* the *obverse* of the very *verbose.* After the *mite* of an *item* that follows, I guarantee that at no *time* will you *emit groans* from your *organs:*

Arty Idol
Watch Ana Gram, and you will see
   Her act inspires *idolatry.*
Please do not come *o tardily,*
   And *dilatory* please don't be.

Adroitly Ana Gram will start
   To alter *daily rot.* She's smart:
A dirty lot, an *oily dart*
   She'll change into the *doily art.*

In the Word Circus, an affinity of meaning often generates an infinity of pleasure. Our arty idol Ana Gram can whirl the word *Episcopal,* and create both *a Popsicle* and *Pepsi-Cola.* She tosses up a *raptor* and down swoops a *parrot.* She can even transform *dyslexia* into DAILY SEX (is that a cause or a cure?) and *antidisestablishmentarianism* into I AM AN ARTIST, AND I BLESS THIS IN ME!

But it is even more fascinating to watch Ana reconfigure words and expressions into other words or statements that bear a meaningful relationship to the base. These significant tandems are called aptagrams — words that anagram into their own synonyms or to uncannily related ideas:

aboard/abroad
abode/adobe
arise/raise
aye/yea
babbling/blabbing
berrybush/shrubbery
brush/shrub

detour/routed
earned/endear
entirety/eternity
evil/vile
ill-used/sullied
impregnate/permeating
insurgent/unresting

it's/'tis
note/tone
nuclear/unclear
rescues/secures
statement/testament
tired/tried
weird/wired

Now for a triple play:

One of the meanings of the adjective *parental* is "pertaining to the influence of a parent." An anagram of *parental* is *paternal,* "pertaining to the influence of the father." *Prenatal,* another anagram of the same word, certainly suggests the influence of the mother.

Next up in this *phase* of anagramazing program are words and phrases that we can *shape* into *heaps* of other meaningful phrases. Thus, the cliché *information super-highway* can become any of the following statements:

OH, WORMY INFURIATING PHRASE.
NEW UTOPIA? HORRIFYING SHAM.
WARNING OF EUPHORIA IS MYTH.
OH-OH, WIRING SNAFU: EMPTY AIR.
AH, INFINITY GREW AMORPHOUS.
HI-HO! YOW! I'M SURFING ARPANET!
WAITING FOR ANY PROMISE, HUH?
O, WORSHIP THE IMAGINARY FUN.
OUR NEW PROFANITY AIMS HIGH.
INSPIRE HUMANITY, WHO GO FAR.
HA! SOMEHOW I PURIFY RANTING.

HEY, IGNORAMUS. WIN PROFIT? HA!
A ROUGH WHIMPER OF INSANITY
I'M ON A HUGE WHISPY RHINO RAFT.
ENORMOUS HAIRY PIG WITH FAN

Two of the longer, more elegantly composed examples of phrase anagramming are:

and

> To be or not to be, that is the question,
> Whether 'tis nobler in the mind to suffer
> The slings and arrows of outrageous fortune,

which reincarnates as:

> In one of the Bard's best-thought-of tragedies,
> Our insistent hero, Hamlet, queries on two fronts
> About how life turns rotten.

Because brevity and levity are the souls of anagrammatical wit, Ana Gram's transformations are more concise. She's *an acrobat* — ACT ON A BAR — as she juggles letters *alphabetically* and laughs, "I PLAY ALL THE ABC." So full of *endearments* is her magic that we bestow TENDER NAMES upon her.

You, dear *patron,* may want NO PART of me. Your *animosity* IS NO AMITY, I know. You may call me a *blatherskite* and think, "THIS BE TALKER." *Ridiculous?* I LUDICROUS. That's *asinine;* it IS INANE. So don't be *mean-spirited* and IN A DISTEMPER. Remember that *villainousness* is AN EVIL SOUL'S SIN. So *bury the hatchet* and BUTCHER THY HATE.

Now that Ana Gram is *enshrined* in your memory, we'll SEND HER IN for a GRAND FINALE — A FLARING END. After *the eyes* THEY SEE and *this ear* IT HEARS her nimble *executions,* she EXITS ON CUE and we exclaim in *unanimity,* "AM IN UNITY! *Mirabile dictu:* I DUB IT A MIRACLE!"

You clearly possess *the sense of humor* and think, "OH, THERE'S SOME FUN!" So for your entertainment we present a parade of meaningful phrase anagrams, the *athletics* of which are LITHE ACTS. Because they are so *appropriate,* they are absolutely A-I, APT, PROPER:

Alcoholics Anonymous	NO SALOONS (HIC!) CALM YOU.
an aisle	IS A LANE
apartheid	A DIRE PATH
atom bombs	A MOB'S TOMB
the Boy Scouts of America	O, IS A BEST MECCA FOR YOUTH
a chain smoker	I'M A HACKER, SON.
considerate	CARE IS NOTED.
conversation	VOICES RANT ON.
a decimal point	I'M A DOT IN PLACE.
departed this life	HE'S LEFT IT, DEAD: R. I. P.
desperation	A ROPE ENDS IT.
disintegration	A ROTTING INSIDE
dormitory	DIRTY ROOM
dynamite	MAY END IT
Fourth of July	JOYFUL FOURTH
gold and silver	GRAND OLD EVILS
Halley's Comet	SHALL YET COME
H.M.S. Pinafore	NAME FOR SHIP
incomprehensible	PROBLEM IN CHINESE
limericks	SLICK RIME
life insurance	IS FINANCE LURE
the Mafioso	O, SHAME OF IT
male chauvinist	HE UNCIVIL AT A MS.
megalomania	A MAIN GOAL: ME
metaphysicians	MYSTICS IN A HEAP
miscalculation	I CALL A MISCOUNT.
monasteries	AMEN STORIES
a near miss	AN AIR MESS
nuclear bombs	CLOBBER US, MAN.
the nudist colony	NO UNTIDY CLOTHES
old England	GOLDEN LAND
the Postmaster-General	HE'S LETTER POST MANAGER.
prosecutors	COURT POSERS
prosperity	IS PROPERTY

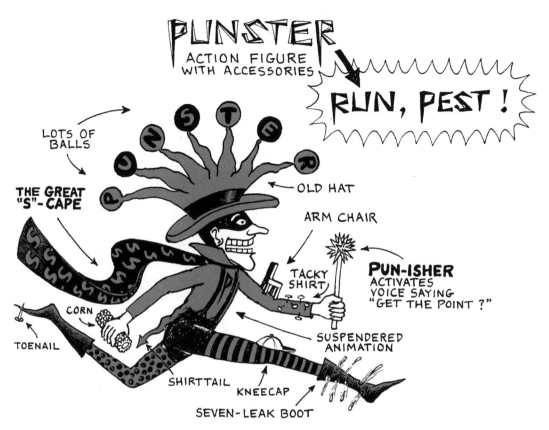

punster	RUN, PEST!
restaurant	RUNS A TREAT.
the rhyming dictionaries	I, RICH METER, AID IN THY SONG.
Russia	I A USSR.
revolution	LOVE TO RUIN
saintliness	LEAST IN SINS
sexual intercourse	RELAX, ENSURE COITUS.
a shoplifter	HAS TO PILFER.
signature	A TRUE SIGN
slot machines	CASH LOST IN 'EM

snooze alarms	ALAS, NO MORE Z'S
solitary confinement	FELONS CRY, "NO MATE IN IT."
Southern California	HOT SUN, OR LIFE IN A CAR
Statue of Liberty	BUILT TO STAY FREE
the Supreme Court	COME TRUST UP HERE.
tantrums	MUST RANT
telegraph	GREAT HELP
television	TV IS ONE LIE.
television set	SEE? IT'S VIOLENT!
the tennis pro	HE IN NET SPORT.
Tower of London	ONE OLD FORT NOW
the unemployed	HELP OUT MY NEED.
United States of America	AN ACUTE STRIFE MADE IT SO.
upholsterers	RESTORE PLUSH
Valentine poem	PEN MATE IN LOVE
Western Union	NO WIRE UNSENT
wild oats	SOW IT, LAD.
X-rated movies	VIDEO SEX MART

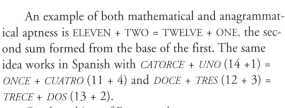

SEE? IT'S VIOLENT!

TELEVISION SET

An example of both mathematical and anagrammatical aptness is ELEVEN + TWO = TWELVE + ONE, the second sum formed from the base of the first. The same idea works in Spanish with *CATORCE + UNO* (14 +1) = *ONCE + CUATRO* (11 + 4) and *DOCE + TRES* (12 + 3) = *TRECE + DOS* (13 + 2).

On the subject of Romance-language anagrams, we give you a classic act — remarkable Latin transposition. Two millennia ago, Pontius Pilate asked Christ: *QUID EST VERITAS?* ("What is truth?") To this Christ did not reply, but the answer was contained in a rearrangement of the question itself: *EST VIR QUI ADEST.* "It is the Man who is here."

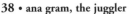

38 • ana gram, the juggler

Some words anagram so prolifically that we can write anagrammatical verse about them:

> VIOLETS
> It's love
> I've lost
> To Evil's
> Vile sot.
> Violet's
> Love 'tis.

or we can versify, diversify, and multiversify a name:

> An idle
> Lead-in
> Ad line:
> DANIEL,
> Nailed
> In deal
> (i.e. land
> In dale),
> Led in a
> Denial
> And lie.

A handful of words are so kaleidoscopic that they turn out to be "perfect anagrams," rearranging themselves to form words that begin with each letter of the original word:

| asp/sap/spa/pa's | ram/arm/mar | rats/arts/tars/tsar/star | tap/apt/pat |
| ate/tea/eat | rat/art/tar | smite/mites/items/times/emits | won/own/now |

Have you ever noticed that the STOP you see on signs yields six different four-letter words that begin with the four letters in STOP?:

> Our landlord *opts* to fill our *pots*
> Until the *tops* flow over.
> Tonight we *stop* upon this *spot,*
> Tomorrow *post* for Dover.

And now, please give a big round of applause to the luminous, the pulsing, the radiating, the brilliant, the scintillating, the twinkling star of our show. Ladies and gentlemen, I give you the word *star:*

Right off, you'll note *s-t-a-r* spells *rats* backwards.

Next, let's move the *s* from front to back and uncover the verb *tars.*

Now we'll twice progress from inside to outside, in the order of 2-1-3-4 and 3-4-2-1, and we derive *tsar* (another spelling of *czar*) and *arts. Star* and its reversal, *rats,* are the only words in English of four letters or more that can perform a double inside-to-outside.

All these combinations produce a perfect anagram:

| star | tsar | tars | arts | rats |

Just for fun, let's promote each letter in *star* by one and see what happens. Voila! We find the word *tubs:*

| s+1=t | t+1=u | a+1=b | r+1=s | =tubs |

A close runner-up to *star* is the gutsy word *intestines.* The first five letters, *intes,* are anagrammed in the second half, *tines.* Both halves are anagrams of *inset,* so we have a word made up of two anagrammatical insets. For a finishing touch, a second body part, with letters in order, is hidden in *intestines.* That word is *testes.*

Third prize goes to *rose,* which comes out smelling like one:

rose   roes   ores   sore   eros

Note that *rose* and *roes* are anagrammed homophones, that *sore* and *eros* are reversals of each other, that *sore* becomes *ores* and *eros rose* when the first letter of each word is moved to the back, and that *roes* becomes *ores* when anagrammed from the inside out — 2-1-3-4.

The converse of the aptagram is the antigram, in which a word or phrase gets rejuggled into another word or phrase that bears a meaning opposite to that of the base. Thus, *astronomers*/MOON STARERS is an aptagram while *astronomers*/NO MORE STARS is an antigram.

I'm *a spellbinder,* not a BLAND SPIELER, and I'm high on *lemonade,* not DEMON ALE, when I tell you that near the end of Ana Gram's juggling act, she is joined by a rather contrary lady — Anti Gram — Ana's favorite among her *versatile relatives.*

Anti Gram's specialty is changing each idea into its anagrammatical opposite.

She converts a *teacher* into a *cheater, mentors* into a *monster,* and an *evangelist* into EVIL'S AGENT. Then she transforms *violence* into NICE LOVE, a *funeral* into REAL FUN, an *anarchist* into an ARCH SAINT, *Satan* into *Santa,* and Satan's *infernos* into *non-fires.*

When your *bedroom* becomes a place of *boredom,* when your *marriage* becomes A GRIM ERA, Anti Gram reshapes your *marital* life into your *martial* life. Then what was *united* becomes *untied;* what was *praised* now causes *despair;* what was once *sunlit* has become an *insult;* what was *medicated* is now *decimated;* and what was *ruthful* is now *hurtful.* What was once *filled* is now *ill-fed;* what was come by *honestly* is now ON THE SLY, and what was worthy of *commendation* the world will now AIM TO CONDEMN, not with a *vote* but with a *veto.* While you were once *defiant,* you have now *fainted.* That to which you once *aspired* now causes you *despair.*

May the parade of antigrams that follows not *fluster* you but make you feel *restful:*

antagonist	NOT AGAINST
diplomacy	MAD POLICY
dormitories	TIDIER ROOMS
gratitude	I GET A TURD
maidenly	MEN DAILY
medical consultations	NOTED MISCALCULATIONS

nominate	I NAME NOT.
old man winter	WARM, INDOLENT
persecuted	DUE RESPECT
a rapscallion	I NO RASCAL, PAL.
saintliness	ENTAILS SINS
spittoon	IT'S NO POT.

Ana Gram and Anti Gram usually twirl balls in a circle, so that each spheroid that starts at the front of the circle gets flipped to the back. The letters of some words can travel the same route. These are looping anagrams — words in which the first letter can be moved from frontword to backword to produce another word.

The most common looping anagrams, and the easiest to construct, are those beginning with *s*. That's why you can change your *spot* and *span* to *pots* and *pans,* simply by moving the *s* from front to back. That's why you can so easily replace your *sword* with *words* so that *words* have then become your *sword. Smile/miles, strap/traps, sexist/exists,* and *shoe/hoes* are other *s* examples. More satisfying are looping anagrams that don't start with *s* and to the eye and the *ear are* especially surprising in their new form:

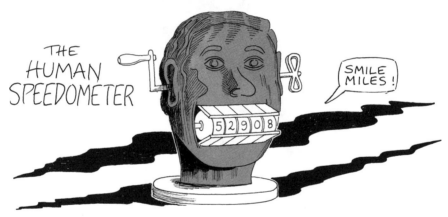

THE HUMAN SPEEDOMETER

5 2 9 0 8

SMILE MILES !

aye/yea	ether/there	lease/easel	rave/aver
car/arc	ethos/those	name/amen	ruse/user
den/end	evil/vile	near/earn	tap/apt
drape/raped	free/reef	nope/open	tough/ought
each/ache	gelatin/elating	now/own	trap/rapt
echoic/choice	grin/ring	plum/lump	trio/riot
eon/one	heart/earth	pram/ramp	wane/anew
esprit/sprite	height/eighth	range/anger	who/how

Animals figure prominently in all this hoopla and loop, ha!

asp/spa	ewe/wee	rhea/hear
drake/raked	flea/leaf	shark/harks
emanate/manatee	low/owl	snail/nails
emit/mite		swine/wines
emus/muse		tan/ant

You'll *grin* at the *ring* of bright letters.
You'll *smile* at the *miles* of fun.
You'll *rove over* anagrams looping.
You'll laugh till you *ache* at *each* one.

A *snail nails pa's asp* in a hot *spa.*
Then a *drake raked* a *flea* off a *leaf.*
A *rhea* will *hear, shark harks, emus muse:*
Will a *manatee emanate* grief?

The *heart* of the *earth* is the looper.
Like an *ape* with a *pea,* you'll soon try it.
When a *stag tags* a *low owl, tan ant,* and *wee ewe,*
The *trio* is likely to *riot.*

The looping of *aide* to *idea* is a delightful transformation because with a single swoop the word triples its syllables. Pluralize *aide* to *aides,* then anagram twice, and you end up with the following progression of syllables:

aides (one syllable)
aside (two syllables)
ideas (three syllables)

Not yet done, because entering the tent are triple super-duper loopers, words that can be looped and then looped again:

ALIEN CLOWNS

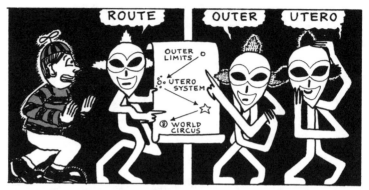

asp/spa/pa's   sear/ears/arse   stable/tables/ablest
emit/mite/item   stripe/tripes/ripest

To complete our pool of looping, swooping anagrams, the Word Circus is proud to present three spectacular triples. In the first triad, the words expand from one syllable to two to three:

route   outer   utero

In the second cluster, the first letter loops to the back. Then the next two letters and then the next three execute the same arc so as to return to the original word. (As all science-fiction fans know, a *terran* is an inhabitant of Earth.) Thus:

terran   errant   ranter   terran

The third grouping is more a progress of meaning:

eat   ate   tea

Ate is the past tense of *eat*. After we *ate*, we washed the whole thing down with *tea*. In this instance, the triple loop returns *eat* to its original base, allowing us to form three word squares:

EAT   ATE   TEA
ATE   TEA   EAT
TEA   EAT   ATE

No wonder that *anagram* is an acronym of *A New, Appropriate, Grandly Rearranged, Alphabetic Message*. No wonder that those who believe in the magical potency of words have hailed *the anagram* as AH, AN ART GEM! and *anagrams* as *ARS MAGNA,* "the great art."

THE pALINDROMEDAry

Back in 1907, one A. C. Pearson asked readers to identify the word described in his little poem:

> A turning point in every day,
>   Reversed I do not alter.
> One half of me says haste away!
>   The other bids me falter.

The answer is *noon.* Half the word is *on* ("haste away!"), and half is *no* ("bids me falter"). Together they form a word that reads the same forwards and backwards.

A palindrome is a word, a *word row,* a sentence, or a longer statement that communicates the same message when the letters of which it is composed are read in reverse order. Palindromes make us exult, *Ah ha! Oh, ho! Hey, yeh!, Yo boy!, Yay!, Wow!, Tut-Tut!, Har-har! Rah-rah!, Heh-heh!,* and *Hoorah! Har! Ooh!* and *Ahem! It's time. Ha!*

A NUT TUNA

If, instead, you are scratching your head and mumbling, *huh?*, cast your gaze on the file of palindromic animals entering the sawdust circle — *a mall llama, a nut tuna, dock cod, dog god, bar crab, tango gnat, E.P.A. ape, reedy deer, Mars ram, worm row, Nehru fur hen, red nag gander, tepee pet,* and a *koala, o.k?* Then you'll *see bees, star rats, sleek eels, sewer ewes, snob big gibbons, snore herons,* and *sad Napa Pandas.*

After a *spider redips* and *dik-diks skid, kid,* we'll *separate tar apes* and then *stack cats,* by placing a *taco cat* upon a base of *senile felines.* Never ever would I *rip a tapir,* nor would I exclaim, "ACROBATS STAB BATS, STAB ORCA" or "TEN ANIMALS I SLAM IN A NET!"

You in the audience may well have come to the Word Circus with your very own palindromic family. There's *mom (a mama)* and *dad (a papa* or *pop)* and *sis* and *tot* and *pup.* And you may have brought along a few of your palindromic friends — *Ada, Anna, Asa, Ava, Bob, Eve, Hannah, Lil, Mim, Nan, Otto,* and *Viv.*

PALINDROMIC FAMILY

DAD   TOT   MOM   SIS   PUP

Even if you're a *dud, kook, boob,* or *poop,* you can find three-, four-, and five-letter palindromes.

In 1941, *radar* was coined to describe a radio device used to locate an object by means of waves reflected from the object and received by the sending unit. The letters in *radar* form not only an acronym ("radio detecting and ranging"), but an especially happy palindromic coinage for the two-way reflection of radio waves. *Radar* is now the best-known word cobbled purposely as a palindrome. There are only a dozen common palindromic words of five letters:

civic	madam	rotor	shahs
kayak	radar	sagas	solos
level	refer	sexes	tenet

Excluding repeated elements such as *heh-heh* and *tut-tut,* the only common six-letter palindromic words are:

pull-up	redder

Four seven-letter palindromes step forward:

deified	reviver
repaper	rotator

The longest fairly common palindromic word in English is the nine-letter *redivider.*

It is to the sentence palindrome that we must turn to discover the most celebrated and adroit exercises in palindromic power and potentiality. Some logolepts claim that the first sentence ever spoken was a palindrome. We are told that the Deity plunged Adam into a deep sleep prior to extracting a rib wherewith to make him a helpmeet. When he awoke, Adam to his amazement found Eve (possessing the first palindromic name, of course) by his side. Having no one to introduce him, he politely bowed and said: MADAM, I'M ADAM.

Name Me Man

Backward and forward, as you will perceive,
   Read Adam's first greeting to dear Mother Eve:
MADAM, I'M ADAM. Now we can conceive
   That her answer was simply: EVE, MAD ADAM, EVE.

Adam may have ribbed us when he said, EVE WAS I ERE I SAW EVE, because Eve was one of his ribs before God extracted it and made her. When he said MADAM IN EDEN, I'M ADAM and NAMED UNDER A BAN, A BARED NUDE MAN, she could have offered any of the following replies:

SIR, I'M IRIS.

EVE IS A SIEVE.

ADAM, I'M ADA.

I'M A MADAM, ADAM, AM I?

EVE, MAIDEN NAME. BOTH SAD IN EDEN? I DASH TO BE MANNED. I AM EVE.

Another famous palindromic sentence was purportedly uttered by Napoleon (in English, of course — so convenient) as he paced the shores of Elba in 1814 — ABLE WAS I ERE I SAW ELBA:

Elba Fable

ABLE WAS I ERE I SAW ELBA,
Napoleon cried like a toy-deprived kid.
Wellington mocked in reply, DID I
DISABLE ELBA'S ID? I DID.

Napoleon might have answered Wellington, ELBA, I'M AMIABLE.

The third, and newest, in the triumvirate of best-known palindromes describes the saga of George Washington Goethals: A MAN! A PLAN! A CANAL! PANAMA!:

Route Canal

There was a man who had a plan
To set a can inside a pan.
He added Al and then a ma —
Built a canal in Panama.
His critics tried to ban him, pan him. Ah!
A MAN! A PLAN! A CANAL! PANAMA!

One of the oldest palindromes appears as a legend on several fountains in Europe, including St. Sophia in Constantinople, Notre Dame in Paris, and St. Martin's in London. The Greek message reads, ΝΙΨΟΝ ΑΝΟΜΗΜΑ, ΜΗ ΜΟΝΑΝ ΟΨΙΝ: *"Wash your sins, not only your face."*

The first recorded sentence palindrome in English comes from the hand of the early-seventeenth-century poet John Taylor: LEWD DID I LIVE & EVIL I DID DWEL. *Dwel* is acceptable seventeenth-century spelling, but the ampersand is a bit of a fudge factor. Still, Taylor's nine-word effort is a promising palindromic path-breaker for the two-way extravaganzas in the Word Circus.

A successful palindromic sentence must make a self-contained and reasonably clear statement and, at the same time, obey the laws of grammar. Palindromes of more than ten thousand words have been recorded in the *Guinness Book of World Records*, but as palindromes expand, their sense gradually evaporates, like the smile on the face of the Cheshire Cat:

> A MAN, A PLAN, A CANOE, PASTA, HEROS, RAJAHS, A COLORATURA, SNIPE, PERCALE, MACARONI, A GAG, A BANANA BAG, A TAN, A TAG, A BANANA BAG AGAIN (OR A CAMEL), A CREPE, PINS, A RUT, A ROLO, CASH, A JAR, SORE HATS, A PEON, A CANAL — PANAMA!

> In Xanadu did Kubla Khan
> A stately palindrome decree.

And in that palindrome lives the Palindromedary — a two-headed, pushme-pullyou camel that looks both ways and meets in the middle.

Ladies and gentlemen! We now present an exclusive interview with the Palindromedary himself, the two-way statement made flesh. This camel is a talking animal smitten with Ailihphilia — the love of palindromes. Thus, whenever the Palindromedary makes a statement, that sentence, SIDES REVERSED, IS the very same sentence.

BARKER: So you're the famous Palindromedary?
PALINDROMEDARY: I, MALE, MACHO, OH, CAMEL AM I.
I see that, despite your fame, you're wearing a name tag. Why?

I, MALE, MACHO, OH, CAMEL AM I.

GATEMAN SEES NAME. GARAGEMAN SEES NAME TAG.

Is it true that people will walk a mile to see your act?

OK, SAY A MILE, MAC. A CAMEL I MAY ASK, O.

Is it true that you were discovered in the Nile region?

CAMEL IN NILE, MAC.

How are you able to speak entirely in palindromes?

SPOT WORD ROW. TOPS!

What kind of word row?

WORD ROW? YA, WOW! TWO-WAY WORD ROW.

I understand that when you insert SIDES REVERSED IS into the middle of a palindrome, it becomes more than twice as long. Please offer an example.

"WORD ROW? YA, WOW! TWO-WAY WORD ROW" SIDES REVERSED IS "WORD ROW? YA, WOW! TWO-WAY WORD ROW."

Let's talk about the Word Circus animal acts. I heard that the trainer said an earful to the flying elephant in your menagerie. What was the trainer's command?

"DUMBO, LOB MUD."

I hear Dan, the lion tamer, is sick in bed and won't get up.

POOR DAN IS IN A DROOP.

Would it cheer Dan up if we dressed him in a colorful outfit?

MIRTH, SIR, A GAY ASSET? NO, DON'T ESSAY A GARISH TRIM.

So there won't be a lion performance today?

NO, SIT! CAT ACT IS ON.

How come? Did Dan take some medicine?

LION OIL.

Have you seen the big cats perform?

OH WHO WAS IT I SAW, OH WHO?

Well, have you seen the big cats in action?

WAS IT A CAR OR A CAT I SAW?

In addition to the big cat act, will we be witnessing performing dogs?

A DOG? A PANIC IN A PAGODA!

If we're not going to see a dog act, where are the dogs kept?

POOCH COOP.

I heard that somebody slipped something into the dog cage.

GOD! A RED NUGGET! A FAT EGG UNDER A DOG!

How did the dog take the prank?

HE GODDAMN MAD DOG, EH.

What happened when you followed the dog act?

DID I STEP ON DOG DOO? GOOD GOD! NO PETS! I DID!

Why aren't the owls performing tonight?

TOO HOT TO HOOT.

And the panda?

PANDA HAD NAP.

And the elk?

ELK CACKLE.

But where are the deer?

DEER FRISK, SIR, FREED.

Is it true that the Word Circus will bring on the clones and that one of the star animal attractions will be that cloned sheep named Dolly?

EWE ERA: WE BAND EWE DNA. BEWARE EWE.

And how successful has your clone act been?

DUAL EWE WE LAUD.

I hear that the animals each get into a cart and have a race around the ring.

TIED, I RIDE IT.

Did you participate in the last animal race?

NO, WE NOT RACE. CART ONE WON.

I understand that the menagerie also includes gnus and zebras.

O GNU, FAR BE ZEBRA FUN! GO!

And did the gnus actually sing the *Star Spangled Banner?*

RISE, NUT! GNUS SUNG TUNE, SIR.

Do the rats join them?

RATS GNASH TEETH; SANG STAR . . .

What about the rumor that one of the gnus is ill?

UNGASTROPERITONITIS: "IS IT I? NOT I," REPORTS A GNU.

What's the problem when you come after the gnu act?

GNU DUNG.

Will we see a yak?

KAY, A RED NUDE, PEEPED UNDER A YAK.

Is it true that Kay rode on your back rather than taking a taxi cab?

HA, BARE BACK RIDER'S RED! IRK CAB ERA, BAH!

Is it also true that you sewed a dress for the kangaroo?

I MADE KANGAROO TUTU. TOO RAG-NAKED AM I.

Speaking of kangaroos, what's your advice on how to train a young wallaby?

LAY A WALLABY BABY BALL AWAY, AL.

What's one of your favorite human circus acts?

TRAPEZE PART.

And what's especially exciting about the trapeze?

TEN ON TRAPEZE PART! NO NET!

No net?

NO TENT NET ON.

Shall we identify and summon the acrobats to perform with the trapeze artists?

TAB OR CALL ACROBAT.

And how do the acrobats train children for their act?

PUPILS ROLL A BALL OR SLIP UP.

I've heard that you occasionally have problems with warts and that you rub your straw on those warts to gain relief.

STRAW? NO! TOO STUPID A FAD. I PUT SOOT ON WARTS.

Have you ever tried fasting to lose weight?

DOC, NOTE. I DISSENT. A FAST NEVER PREVENTS A FATNESS. I DIET ON COD.

So what did you emphasize in your diet?

DESSERTS I STRESSED.

Desserts were at the center of your diet?

I SAW DESSERTS. I'D NO LEMONS, ALAS, NO MELON; DISTRESSED WAS I.

Why do you have a no-smoking policy at the Word Circus?

CIGAR? TOSS IT IN A CAN. IT IS SO TRAGIC.

So every single cigar and cigarette has been thrown out?

NO TRACE. NOT ONE CARTON.

Not one?

BUT SAD EVA SAVED A STUB.

Eva?

EVA CAN, IN A CAVE.

Can you point out Eva for us?

EVA, WE'RE HERE. WAVE.

You seem truly excited about the Word Circus.

AVID AS A DIVA.

Are there any acts that you would get rid of?

DUDE, NOT ONE DUD.

But what do you say to those who contend that the circus can't survive as an art form?

NO! IT CAN! ACTION!

Can the corporate world save the circus?

NO, IT IS OPPOSED. ART SEES TRADE'S OPPOSITION.

So the business world is not for you?

NO, IT'S A BOZO BASTION.

Will the Word Circus continue to evolve?

ARE WE NOT DRAWN ONWARD, WE FEW, DRAWN ONWARD TO NEW ERA?

Mr. Palindromedary. We thank you for such a scintillating two-way interview. Is it true that you are the only animal who can speak intelligibly in palindromes?

YES, THAT'S TRUE. ALL OTHER ANIMALS SAY THINGS LIKE

Ladies and gentlemen! We trust that we've relieved any Aibohphobia, any fear of palindromes that you might have harbored. On the hooves of that palindramatic exchange, feast your eyes on fifty of the best modern palindromic statements, arranged in order of increasing length:

I PREFER PI.

MIX A MAXIM.

IF I HAD A HI-FI

A GOY DID YOGA.

RISE TO VOTE SIR!

BOSNIA: PAIN, SOB.

SO MANY DYNAMOS.

LID OFF A DAFFODIL

NEVER ODD OR EVEN.

TOO BAD I HID A BOOT.

SPACE SUIT (I USE CAPS)

TRACI TORE EROTIC ART.

NIAGARA, O ROAR AGAIN.

AH, SATAN SEES NATASHA.

WELFARE MOM ERA FLEW.

MA IS AS SELFLESS AS I AM.

EMIL ASLEEP PEELS A LIME.

STELLA WON NO WALLETS.

NURSE, I SPY GYPSIES. RUN!

MAY A BANANA NAB A YAM?

DRAW PUPIL'S LIP UPWARD.

A SLUT NIXES SEX IN TULSA.

SIT ON A POTATO PAN, OTIS.

DRAB AS A FOOL, ALOOF AS A BARD.

BOSS SAY, "D.N.A.!" CANDY-ASS S.O.B.

YO! BOTTOMS UP! U.S. MOTTO, BOY!

GOLF? NO SIR. PREFER PRISON FLOG.

ELK CITY, KANSAS, IS A SNAKY TICKLE.

DIANA SAW DR. AWKWARD WAS AN AID.

"NAOMI, SEX AT NOON TAXES," I MOAN.

LIVE ON EVASIONS? NO, I SAVE NO EVIL.

SIR, I DEMAND I AM A MAID NAMED IRIS.

RETTA HAS ADAMS AS MAD AS A HATTER.

GO HANG A SALAMI. I'M A LASAGNA HOG.

EGAD, A BASE TONE DENOTES A BAD AGE.

SIR, A FAST ANISE MADE DAME SIN AT SAFARIS.

STOP! MURDER US NOT, TONSURED RUMPOTS!

"DO NINE MEN INTERPRET?" "NINE MEN," I NOD.

MARGE, LET A MOODY BABY DOOM A TELEGRAM.

ANNE, I VOTE MORE CARS RACE ROME-TO-VIENNA.

NOW NED, I AM A MAIDEN NUN; NED, I AM A MAIDEN WON.

A NEW ORDER BEGUN, A MORE ROMAN AGE BRED ROWENA.

I MAIM NINE MEN IN SAGINAW; WAN I GAS NINE MEN IN MIAMI.

BARCLAY ORDERED AN OMELETTE, LEMONADE, RED ROYAL CRAB.

TELL A PLATE MAN ON A MOROSE DAMSITE BY ME TO NOTE MY BET
IS MADE SO ROMAN ON A METAL PALLET.

The longest name ever to be embedded in a graceful palindrome
appears in:

DRAW, O CONSTANTINOPLE! HELP ON IT! NAT'S NO COWARD!

The immortal J. Lindon and Leigh Mercer had a knack for embedding
very long words in palindromic statements:

NAMED UNDENOMINATIONALLY REBEL, I RILE BERYL? LA NO! I TAN. I'M, O NED, NUDE, MAN!

PUSILLANIMITY OBSESSES BOY TIM IN "ALL IS UP."

PUSILLANIMITY
OBSESSES BOY TIM
IN "ALL IS UP."

Back in March 1866, there appeared in *Our Young Folks* magazine an extraordinary Latin-English pairing, created by James C. P., that reads forward in English and backward in Latin. The reverse pair not only make sense in both directions, but retain the same meaning in both languages and both directions!:

ANGER? 'TIS SAFE NEVER. BAR IT! USE LOVE!

EVOLES UT IRA BREVE NEFAS SIT; REGNA!

The literal translation of the Latin is "Rise up, in order that your anger may be but a brief madness; control it!"

A word-unit palindrome is a sentence or sequence of sentences that, word for word, reads the same forwards and backwards. Could it be, for example, that the Domino Theory, so prominent during the Vietnam War, has now shriveled and become the TIC TAC TOE TACTIC?

Ladies and gentlemen, cross your eyes as you read the best of word-unit palindromes, noting that the first statement is cobbled entirely from words that are themselves palindromic:

DID HANNAH PEEP? HANNAH DID.
SO PATIENT A DOCTOR TO DOCTOR A PATIENT SO.
BORES ARE PEOPLE THAT SAY THAT PEOPLE ARE BORES.
STOUT AND BITTER PORTER DRINKS PORTER, BITTER AND STOUT.
FIRST LADIES RULE THE STATE, AND STATE THE RULE — "LADIES FIRST!"
GIRL, BATHING ON BIKINI, EYEING BOY, FINDS BOY EYEING BIKINI ON BATHING GIRL.
YOU CAN CAGE A SWALLOW CAN'T YOU, BUT YOU CAN'T SWALLOW A CAGE, CAN YOU?

William Shakespeare planted a pair of word-unit palindromes in some of his most resonant passages in *Macbeth:*

> Paddock calls — anon! —
> FAIR IS FOUL, AND FOUL IS FAIR.
> Hover through the fog and filthy air.

Perhaps even more famous is Alexandre Dumas' ALL FOR ONE AND ONE FOR ALL.

Close kin to the palindrome is the semordnilap. Take a good look at the word *semordnilap,* and you'll find that it is *palindromes* spelled backwards. While a palindromic word conveys the same message left to right and right to left, a semordnilap becomes a new word when spelled in reverse:

bats/stab	ergo/ogre	rebut/tuber
decal/laced	faced/decaf	snug/guns
deliver/reviled	gulp/plug	stinker/reknits
devil/lived	keel/leek	straw/warts
diaper/repaid	mined/denim	warder/redraw
drab/bard	part/trap	wolf/flow
drawer/reward	pool/loop	won ton/not now

In 1876, these two semordnilapic conundrums appeared in England:

> I glad the eye in sweet Spring time
>   On England's soil, when brought to view;
> Reverse me, in another clime
>   I charm eye, nose, and palate too.

* * *

> If forward you read me, a bird I shall be,
>   Much sought for some time in the year;
> Now backward, a quadruped soon you will see,
>   And my color will likewise appear.

The solutions are *May/yam* and *gander/nag, red.*

Sometimes the reversal is especially meaningful. For instance, a number of people feel that the sport is called *golf* not just because all the other four-letter words were used up, but because *golf* spelled backwards is *flog.* Others insist that *boss* is spelled *b-o-s-s* because your boss is a backward double *s-o-b!*

Ladies and gentlemen! Entering the sawdust circle, bass ackwards of course, are more examples of backward logic:

One is liable to find *amor* in *Roma.*
Theater lovers are *avid* about a *diva.*
During an *embargo,* each article withheld seems to say, "O GRAB ME!"
Eros spelled backwards gives you an idea of how it affects beginners.
Harpo Marx was famous for his silence; *Oprah* Winfrey is famous for her conversation.
Bud *Selig* and Warren *Giles* have been high-ranking baseball commissioners.

A DARK MOOD PRESAGES DOOM.

A *leper* tends to *repel.*
A dark *mood* presages *doom.*
To Captain *Nemo* a giant squid was an ill *omen.*
It's apt that a *pat* is a kind of *tap.*
Pees often *seep.*
We are likely to *rail* at a *liar.*
State in reverse is *etats,* its own plural in French.
War is a *raw* experience for humankind.
A *wonk* will *know* a lot about a certain subject.

No wonder that *palindrome* is an acronym for *Particularly Adroit Language Image Nicely Duplicating Reversed-Order Message Exactly.*

No wonder that, antigrammatically, a *palindrome* is anything but a *random pile* of letters. Rather a *palindrome* is, anagrammatically, ALMOND RIPE and proudly proclaims, "I MODERN PAL."

No wonder that palindromes are *summus,* palindromic Latin for "the highest," and exclaim "SPLENDOR AM I!"

BIG-NAME

Throughout the history of the circus, famous names have attracted huge audiences: the aerialists Jules Leotard, Alfredo Cordona, and Lillian Letzel; Buffalo Bill and Annie Oakley of the Wild West Circus; the juggler Enrico Rastelli; and the flying Wallendas, the Guerrero family, Bird Millman, and Cabot Colleano on the tightrope.

The wild animal trainers Clyde Beatty, Alfred Court, and Gunther Goebel-Williams; the clowns Popono, Coco, Holloway, Auriol, Joey Grimaldi, Grock, Yankee Dan Rice, Emmet Kelly, and Otto Griebling; the bareback riders May Wirth, the Christianis, and the Hannefor family; and the bandmaster Merle Evans have lit the history of the circus.

And great beasts, such as the gorilla Gargantua; the elephants Jumbo, Big Bingo, Fantoosh, Gunga, and King Tusk; Thor the White Rhino; Kenny the Leopard; and Dickie the Giraffe, have kept the turnstiles turning with style.

The name is the game —
and the game is the name —
in the Word Circus, too.

ACTS

As Shakespeare's Juliet never asked, "What's in an anagrammed name?" We're about to find out. And speaking of the Bard, another question is: Did William Shakespeare really write the works of Shakespeare, or was it some other fellow named Edward de Vere, Philip Sidney, Queen Elizabeth, Walter Raleigh, Christopher Marlowe, or Francis Bacon (a natural ham)?

Clearly, it must have been William Shakespeare who gave the world all those plays, sonnets, and lyrics. Surely, it was William Shakespeare, that darling of critics and playgoers alike, who changed the world by changing the word. We know this because the Bard is the only writer who lights up the literary firmament with four luminous anagrams of his name:

> I SWEAR HE'S LIKE A LAMP.
> WE ALL MAKE HIS PRAISE.
> HAS WILL A PEER, I ASK ME?
> AH, I SPEAK A SWELL RIME.

How true: Peerless Will Shakespeare shines throughout the ages, accumulating plaudits for his superb poetry. And we could add I AM A WEAKISH SPELLER to the list, given the myriad of ways that William Shakespeare spelled his last name.

Does Elvis Presley live on so powerfully because ELVIS LIVES is an anagram of itself? Does The Doors lead singer, Jim Morrison, remain in our minds and hearts because MR. MOJO RISIN', in the classic song "L.A. Woman," is a transposition of his name? Is the spiky-haired, spiky-personalitied Bart Simpson so named because reversing the middle two letters brings forth *Brat?*

For centuries, puzzlers have been anagramming the names of the famous and infamous:

Adam and Eve	DAD, EVEN A MA
Alexander the Great	GENERAL TAXED EARTH.
Marie Antoinette	TEAR IT, MEN. I ATONE.
Napoleon Bonaparte	NO, APPEAR NOT ON ELBA!
Eddie Cantor	ACTOR INDEED!
Andrew Dice Clay	DARE A LEWD CYNIC.
Tom Cruise	SO I'M CUTER.
Madam Curie	RADIUM CAME.
Charles Dickens	CHEER SICK LANDS.
Robert Dole	ELDER ROBOT
Clint Eastwood	OLD WEST ACTION
Albert Einstein	TEN ELITE BRAINS
Ralph Waldo Emerson	PERSON WHOM ALL READ
Alec Guinness	GENUINE CLASS
Adolf Hitler	HATED FOR ILL
Oliver Wendell Holmes	HE'LL DO IN MELLOW VERSE.

Martin Luther King	LINE MARKING TRUTH
Richard Lederer	RIDDLER REACHER
Henry Wadsworth Longfellow	WON HALF THE NEW WORLD'S GLORY
Jackie Mason	A MANIC JOKES.
Piet Mondrian	I PAINT MODERN.
Horatio Nelson	LO, A NATION'S HERO
Florence Nightingale	FLIT ON, CHEERING ANGEL!
Jacqueline Kennedy Onassis	IS AS QUEENLY ON DECK IN JEANS
Eleanor Roosevelt	ROLE: TO SERVE ALONE
Dante Gabriel Rossetti	GREATEST BORN IDEALIST
Salman Rushdie	DARE SHUN ISLAM.
Sir Walter Scott	LAST SCOT WRITER

Beverly Sills	SILVERY BELLS
Stephen Sondheim	DEMON! HE PENS HITS!
Margaret Thatcher	MEG, THE ARCH TARTAR
Henry David Thoreau	A VERY HIDDEN AUTHOR
Oscar Wilde	I LACE WORDS.

Would that Ross Perot had been elected president of the United States, for his name yields two exquisitely natural anagrams:

| Ross Perot | SORE SPORT |
| H. Ross Perot | SHORT POSER |

Presidential anagramming has been indulged in for more than a century. Some work better grammatically than others; some are more appropriate to the president, some less telling. For example, it is interesting to note that, until 1992, only president Richard Milhous Nixon's name contained the letters of the word *criminal*. Now we have a second president with a *criminal* embedment — *William Jefferson Clinton.*

What's in a president's name? Plenty, when you start anagramming the monikers of our twentieth-century chief executives:

Theodore Roosevelt	LOVED HORSE; TREE, TOO.
William Howard Taft	A WORD WITH ALL: I'M FAT.
Woodrow Wilson	O LORD, SO NOW WWI.
Warren Gamaliel Harding	REAL WINNER? HIM A LAGGARD.
Calvin Coolidge	LOVE? A COLD ICING.
Herbert Clark Hoover	O, HARK, CLEVER BROTHER.
Franklin Delano Roosevelt	ELEANOR, KIN, LAST FOND LOVER
Harry S. Truman	RASH ARMY RUNT
Dwight David Eisenhower	HE DID VIEW THE WAR DOINGS.
John Fitzgerald Kennedy	ZING! JOY DARKEN, THEN FLED.
Lyndon Baines Johnson	NO NINNY, HE'S ON JOB LADS.
Richard Milhous Nixon	HUSH — NIX CRIMINAL ODOR!
Gerald Rudolph Ford	A RUDER LORD; GOLF PH.D.

JAMES
EARL
CARTER
◦
A RARE
CALM
JESTER

James Earl Carter	A RARE, CALM JESTER
Ronald Wilson Reagan	INSANE ANGLO WARLORD
George Bush	HE BUGS GORE.
William Jefferson Clinton	JILTS NICE WOMEN; IN FOR FALL.

In honor of our first president, we present a stately sonnet. Each line is an anagram of the title, yet the lines are cast in reasonable meter and each couplet rhymes! The sonneteer is one David Shulman, and the poem appeared in the June 1936 issue of *Enigma*:

Washington Crossing the Delaware
A hard, howling, tossing, water scene:
Strong tide was washing hero clean.
"How cold!" Weather stings as in anger,
O silent night shows war ace danger!

The cold waters swashing on in rage.
Redcoats warn slow his hint engage.
When general's star action wish'd "Go!"
He saw his ragged continentals row.

Ah, he stands — sailor crew went going
And so this general watches rowing.
He hastens. Winter again grows cold;
A wet crew gain Hessian stronghold.

George can't lose war with 's hands in.
He's astern — so, go alight, crew, and win!

A number of lesser-known people happen to have anagrammed names. Ross Eckler electronically riffled through more than ninety million names in U.S. telephone directories to find multiple examples of the following listings, in which each first name rearranges to form each last name:

Albert Bartel
Amy May
Arnold Roland
Dale Deal
Debra Bader
Debra Beard
Earl Lear
Edna Dane
Edna Dean
Eric Rice
Erich Reich
Gary Gray

Leah Hale
Lena Lane
Leon Noel
Lewis Wiles
Lionel O'Neill
Marc Cram
Neal Lane
Norma Moran
Roland Arnold
Romeo Moore
Ronald Arnold
Ronald Roland

Hurry! Hurry! Hurry! Now that you've explored the anagrammatical wonders of names, it's time to enter the great Palindrome of Appellations.

You, gentle patron, are a very special person because you will almost certainly live in two palindromic years, ones in which the numbers read the same both forwards and backwards.

We are in the middle of an eleven-year span between the palindromic years 1991 and 2002. The last time a smaller hiatus occurred was between the years 999 and 1001. Then for almost an entire millennium, we had to wait 110 years from one palindromic year to the next: 1001, 1111, 1221, 1331, 1441, 1551, 1661, 1771, 1881, 1991. Only one out of every two billion of us human beings lives to the age of 116. Thus, hardly anyone during the past millennium has ever lived through two palindromic years.

Now there's an excellent chance that you, O valued member of our audience, will accomplish that feat. After the year 2002, we'll resume the 110-year intervals — 2002, 2112, 2222, 2332, and so on. Indeed, we won't attain another eleven-year spacing till 2992-3003!

ROLAND   RONALD
ARNOLD   ARNOLD

In 1991, what seventeen-year-old woman supplanted Steffi Graf to become the top-ranked tennis player in the world? The answer is Monica *Seles*. That is, a woman with a palindromic last name became the world's best tennis player in a palindromic year. You might call the coincidence a self-fulfilling moniker.

What's in a palindromic name? A great deal, if you will now turn your attention to the palindromeda strain of appellations.

Basketball star and flake *Dennis Rodman* is infamous for his amoral and unpredictable behavior — everything from stomping a courtside photographer to dressing in drag. All this is not so surprising when you realize that *Dennis* is a semordnilap of *sinned* and *Rodman* is an anagram of *random*.

In 1996, "Gangsta Rapper" *Tupac* Shakur was fatally shot at the age of twenty-five. Would he have lived less recklessly if he had realized that his first name was *caput* spelled backwards?

The surname of Panamaniacal strongman Manuel *Noriega* is made from two semordnilaps of the words *iron age* — a sure indication that the dictator was too far behind the times.

Cambodian dictator *Pol Pot* had a tendency to *lop* off the *top* of people.

Palindromes rarely incorporate the names of well-known people. It's usually the fictitious Dennis and Edna who sinned, not John F. Kennedy and Marilyn Monroe:

DENNIS AND EDNA SINNED.

And they're not the only transgressors:

DENNIS, NELL, EDNA, MARVA, LEON, NEDRA, ANITA, ROLF, NORA, ALICE, CAROL, LEO, JANE, REED, DENA, DALE, BASIL, RAE, PENNY, LANA, DAVE, DENNY, LENA, IDA, BERNADETTE, BEN, RAY, LILA, NINA, JO, IRA, MARA, ANNE, NORAH, SELA, GAIA, MABLE, MINA, RAE, BARBA, ROLLO, PAM, ADA, FLORA, TINA, NELL, ETTA, MARY, META, NOEL, FLO, DOT, TOM, ASA, RITA, NAN, IDA, TED, ANA, ESME, HANNAH, EM, SEAN, ADE, TAD, INA, NAT, IRA, SAM, OTTO, DOLF, LEO, NATE, MYRA, MATT, ELLEN, ANITA, ROLF, ADAM, APOLLO, RABRA, BEA, RANI, MELBA, MAIA, GALE, SHARON, ENNA, ARA, MARIO, JAN, INA, LILY, ARNE, BETTE, DAN, REBA, DIANE, LYNN, ED, EVA, DANA, LYNNE, PEARL, ISABEL, ADA, NED, DEE, RENA, JOEL, LORA, CECIL, AARON, FLORA, TINA, ARDEN, NOEL, AVRAM, AND ELLEN SINNED!

Dennis and Edna and their carnal gang join the moaning Naomi, the lime-peeling Emil, the maiden-winning Ned, and Otis, with his penchant for sitting on potato pans, among the no-name palindromes.

Lament not, ladies and gents, for a rich trove of famous names reposes in the canon of palindromes. First, we'll look at single names only:

SIS, IS ISIS ISIS?
POSE AS AESOP.
SAD, I'M MIDAS
XERXES: EX-REX
OJ: NAB A BANJO.
Y'ALL, I'M MILLAY.
NO, I DID DIDION
RED LENIN ELDER

VANNA, WANNA V?
SUIT NO PONTIUS.
I, PLATO, TOTAL PI.
CAMUS SEES SUMAC.
CAIN: A MONOMANIAC
BAR ARAFAT, A FAR ARAB.
ROB A GEM? ME? GABOR?
I YAM POPEYE, POP, MAY I?
ERROL'S PAL SLAPS LORRE.
HELL, ATTILA LIT TALL, EH?
GOD, ASTOR TROTS A DOG.
LION TO OZ: "ZOOT 'N' OIL."
MAN, OPRAH'S SHARP ON A.M.
NORIEGA CASTS A CAGE: IRON.
O, GERONIMO, NO MINOR EGO.
DRAW, O CAESAR. ERASE A COWARD.

YAP! YAP!

GOD, ASTOR TROTS A DOG.

RAW-FIST CAPONE: "NO PACTS IF WAR!"

NO HAM CAME, SIR. RISE, MACMAHON.

MANET TASTES SAP ASSETS AT TEN A.M.

DEPARDIEU, GO RAZZ A ROGUE I DRAPED.

EH? DID ZORRO GIVE VIGOR, ROZ? DID HE?

SUMS ARE NOT SET AS A TEST ON ERASMUS.

SET ARC. OSTRACIZE FEZ. I CART SOCRATES.

SIS, ASK COSTNER TO NOT RENT SOCKS "AS IS."

NOW ALL ARE NEGATIVE, EVITA; GENERAL LAW ON.

MAD ZEUS, NO LIVE DEVIL, LIVED EVIL ON SUEZ DAM.

Focusing on United States history, we give you an unprecedented presentation of presidential palindromes:

NOT NIL; CLINTON.

I'M A BUSH SUB, AM I

WANT FAT TAFT? NAW.

NO SIRRAH, HARRISON!

NO, SID, AM I MADISON?

NO X IN MR. R. M. NIXON.

NOW RELY — TYLER WON.

GOD! ADAMS IS MAD — A DOG!

RETRACTING, I SIGN IT CARTER.

TO LAST, CARTER RETRACTS A LOT.

O, NOTE: VOTE! OR NO MONROE TO VETO. NO!

RAW? TAP MARTY VAN BUREN. ONE RUB: NAVY TRAMP AT WAR.

Two prolific palindromic single names have spawned a spate of palindromes. The first is Madonna, the stage name for Madonna Louise Ciccone:

PLAN NO DAMN MADONNA L.P.
RISE, MADONNA. MAN NO DAME, SIR.
YAWN. MADONNA FAN. NO DAMN WAY!

The other name belongs to the man who, while putting the world between Iraq and a hard place, became the mother of all palindromes:

DRAT SADDAM, A MAD DASTARD.
A RED RAT, SADDAM. A MAD DASTARD ERA.
DRAT SADDAM, ALL ITS EVIL ALIVE. STILL A MAD DASTARD.

A few first and last names are naturally palindromic. U Nu was Premier of Burma until he was deposed in 1958 and later became an internationally known Asian diplomat during the 1960s. Lon Nol became Premier of Cambodia in 1970.

Robert "Bob" Trebor was a talk show host and announcer on San Francisco's KGO radio. The Sununus have dominated New Hampshire poli-

tics for decades, where oft has been heard the palindromic yawp NOW
SUNUNU'S WON!

Anuta Catuna of Romania came in first in the 1996 New York City
Marathon. At the finish line, she might well have cried, "MA, I WON! NOW I
AM!" Then, because of the literal meaning of the word *palindrome* ("run for-
ward and backward"), she could have run the course over again, backward!

But most names must be dexterously reversed and divided in order to fit
into a palindromic statement, especially when both first and last names, or
initials, get in on the fun:

OH NO! DON HO!

ONO OK, O YOKO ONO?

R. E. LEE: POTATO PEELER

TO IDI AMIN: I'M A IDIOT.

LISA BONET ATE NO BASIL.

'TIS BURL IVES AS EVIL RUBS IT.

TARZAN RAISED DESI ARNAZ' RAT.

LIAM NEESON DID NO SEEN MAIL.

WON'T I, PATTI PAGE, GAP IT, TAP IT NOW?

NO, MEL GIBSON IS A CASINO'S BIG LEMON.

ED, I SAW HARPO MARX RAM OPRAH W. ASIDE.

E. BORGNINE DRAGS DAD'S GARDENING ROBE.

HAKEEM OLAJUWON'S NOW UJA! LO! MEEK! AH!

HE'S A CARAMEL IN NIGER, DAKAR — A BUM IN SOHO — HOSNI MUBARAK, A DREG IN NILE MARACAS, EH?

Now the center ring spotlight falls on two much longer palindromes,
each of which embeds double names with amazing grace:

ENOLA MEGATONS — A LONE DETONATOR'S BOMB. MOBS ROT; A NOTED ENOLA'S NOT A GEM ALONE.

and:

T. ELIOT, TOP BARD, NOTES PUTRID TANG EMANATING, IS SAD. I'D ASSIGN IT A NAME: "GNAT DIRT."
UPSET ON DRAB POT TOILET.

Last, but far from least in our big-name show, here's a parade of brand-new palindromes — well known brand names that work two ways, sort of the way *a Toyota* does:

Aziza (cosmetic line)
Civic (Honda automobile)
Elle (magazine)
Eve (cigarettes)
Mum (deodorant)
Noxon (silver polish)

Pep (cereal)
See's (candies)
S.O.S. (scouring pads)
Tat (insect repellent)
TNT (TV channel)
Xanax (sedative)

Are we being sneaky to include *Adida?* If the shoe fits, please wear it. And if the diaper fits, you'll be repaid with a *Pull-Up,* a single item from a box of Huggies Pull-Ups.

And there's also *ZOONOOZ,* a magazine published by the Zoological Society of San Diego since 1920. In capital letters, *ZOONOOZ* is an extraordinary title because it is palindromic, palindromic in a mirror, palindromic upside down, and palindromic upside down in a mirror.

But the quintessential brand-name palindrome belongs to a stock (bouillon) cube popular throughout the United Kingdom — OXO, a palindrome in at least ten ways. Like *ZOONOOZ,* OXO appears as a palindrome right side up, upside down, and both ways in a mirror. But unlike *ZOONOOZ,* each letter in OXO, whether upper- or lower-cased, is itself a palindrome when sliced horizontally or vertically, yielding six additional palindromes (three times two):

> OXO! OXO! boiling bright
> In the forests of the night,
> What immortal hand or eye
> Could frame thy fearful symmetry?

A while back, one couldn't avoid advertisements for *Serutan,* a patent medicine whose name was designed to spell *Natures* backwards. A number of brand names also spell words in reverse, even if they weren't designed to do that.

We doubt that the manufacturers of *RedRum* coconut rum realized — as all who have read or seen *The Shining* know — that *red rum* is a semordnilap for *murder*. Do the manufacturers of *Evian* mineral water think that we're being *naive* when we imbibe their product?

Here's our assembly line of brand-new semordnilaps:

Ban (deodorant)/nab
Dial (soap)/laid
Era (detergent)/are
Gem (razor blades)/meg
Lever (soap)/revel
Mad (magazine)/dam
Pacer (automobile)/recap
Pam (cooking oil)/map
Pine Sol (cleaning liquid)/lose nip
Ris (paper products)/sir
Sega (video games)/ages
Seiko (watches)/Okies
Spackle (wall filler)/elk caps

Spam (canned meat)/maps
Star Mart (stores)/tram rats
Strata (golf balls)/at arts
Strohs (beer)/shorts
Tab (cola)/bat
Tang (powdered drink)/gnat
Tide (detergent)/edit
Time (magazine)/emit
Tip Top (bread)/pot pit
Tulsa (gasoline)/a slut
Tums (antacid tablets)/smut
Wal-Mart (stores)/tram-law
Wang (computers)/gnaw

And how's this for a two-for-one bargain?: *Avon* (cosmetics) is a reversal of *Nova* (an automobile manufactured by Chevrolet), and *Kool* (cigarettes) mirrors *Look* (a formerly popular magazine) spelled backwards.

One last commercial semordnilap: Up until 1970, if you had been driving on West Miner Street in Yreka, California, you would have come upon the Yreka Bakery. Alas, that bakery is now closed, but its semordnilapic spirit remains aquiver. The premises are now occupied by the Yrella Gallery.

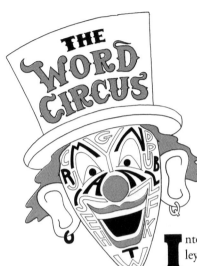

CLOWN CARS

Into the circus ring wobbles a parti-colored, motley Volkswagen. The pint-size vehicle jerks to a stop. Doors open and out spill not one, not two, but up to a dozen bouncing, jouncing, flouncing, pouncing clowns — clowns whose two lips are blue lips, whose tummies are pillowy and trousers are billowy — saggy, baggy pants held up by giant safety pins.

Out tumbles a jumble of vagabond clowns in outsized clumsy shoes; Auguste clowns with high white faces; dwarf clowns in checkered coats; midget clowns in plaid jackets; bewhiskered character clowns who tear a wardrobe to tatters; stilted clowns, broad-striped, polka-dotted, derby-hatted, great-shod; straw-haired clowns, bubble-nosed, great-eyed, gap-toothed, flap-eared. Mimes, jesters, motleys, Pagliacchis, Merry Andrews, harlequinades, pierrots, knockabouts, buffoons, mountebanks, tramps, hobos, zanies, Scaramouches, Cascadeurs.

Around the ring scamper bucket-sloshing, custard-throwing, horn-tooting, pistol-squirting, plunger-pushing, bottom-kicking, nose-twisting, slap-sticking clowns — the funniest, saddest sight you've ever seen. We look in the mirror of a clown's face, and we see the eternal fool lurking in all of us — our scapegoat, our critic, our healer, our selves.

How can so many clowns fit into such a tiny vehicle?
Some are midgets, and others have learned to fold their bodies
so that they don't take up much room.

Like a clown car, words that seem to be single words hide
within them other words. *Indiscrimination* is written as a single
word but divides into seven chain-linked words — IN, DISC, RIM,
IN, AT, I, and ON. *Ampersand* cleverly divides into three words with a pro-
gressive number of letters — AM PER SAND. *Abracadabra* magically transforms into A BRA, CAD, A BRA!

In the game of charades, we act out a big word by dividing it into smaller words. Similarly, a charade word is one in which the larger word can be
divided into smaller parts that are themselves words. We'll start the charading by parading some animals that are made of many parts:

beaver	BE AVER	loon	LO ON
buffaloes	BUFF ALOES	parrot	PAR ROT
donkey	DON KEY	pinto	PIN TO
flamingo	FLAMING O	robin	ROB IN
goat	GO AT	sparrow	SPAR ROW
heron	HER ON	stallion	STALL ION
herring	HER RING	toad	TO AD
kitten	KIT TEN	wombat	WOMB AT

A few circus creatures also join the charade by revealing animals within
animals:

antelope	ANT ELOPE
meadowlark	MEAD OW LARK/MEAD OWL ARK
pigeon	PIG EON

Many non-bestial words divide themselves into fascinating segments. Don't let charade words *bewilder* you. Just BE WILDER about how you look at them:

abundance	A BUN DANCE	molesting	MOLE STING
artichoke	ART: I CHOKE.	mustache	MUST ACHE
atrophy	A TROPHY	office	OFF ICE
attendance	AT TEN, DANCE.	oftentimes	OF TEN TIMES
awesome	A WE SO ME	paltry	PAL TRY
bowlegged	BOWL EGGED	panache	PAN ACHE
detergent	DETER GENT	pleasure	PLEA SURE
discovery	DISCO VERY	prosecute	PROSE CUTE
impact	IMP, ACT!	pumpkin	PUMP KIN
important	I'M PORT ANT.	puppet	PUP PET
legends	LEG ENDS	sunglasses	SUNG LASSES
manicure	MAN, I CURE.	tapestry	TAPES TRY
massacre	MASS ACRE	weeknights	WEE KNIGHTS

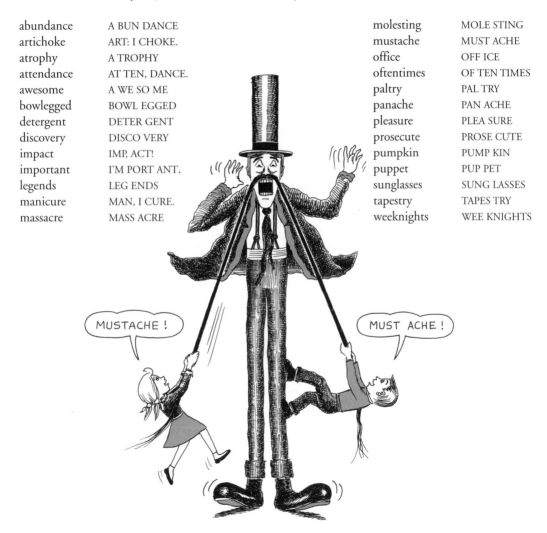

MUSTACHE !

MUST ACHE !

Dr. Samuel Johnson created a charade in the first stanza of his punderful verse:

Many a pun and riddle raids the concept of charades. Some retain the original spellings; some don't:

*When is a door not a door?
 When it's ajar (a jar).

*Don't *assume* because it makes an ass out of you and me.

*What's the cost of earrings for pirates?
 A buck an ear.

*What did the acorn exclaim when it grew up?
 "Gee, Ah'm a tree!"

*I scream for ice cream.

*Why is *O* the only vowel we hear?
Because the rest are inaudible (in audible).

*Fire is the forest's prime evil.

*Triumph is simply *umph* added to *try.*

*What do you call two people who each have a Ph.D.?
A paradox (pair of docs).

*What's the difference between a one-winged angel and a two-winged angel?
It's a matter of a pinion.

*The word *politics* is formed from *poly,* which means "many" (as in *polygon, polyglot, polytheism,* and *polygamy*), and *tics,* which are blood-sucking parasites.

*What's the difference between a weatherman and a corpulent bladder expert?
One is a meteorologist; the other is a meaty urologist.

*I tried to impress my boyfriend with my puns, but no pun in ten did.

*In the Word Circus, all the letter play is in tents.

Charade riddles came into fashion in the late eighteenth century. In these posers, the numbers refer to the syllables in each answer:

> My first is company.
> My second shuns company.
> My third assembles company.
> My whole amuses company.

The answer is *conundrum: co* stands for *"company"*; a *nun* "shuns company"; a *drum* "assembles company" — and a *conundrum* "amuses company."

Now solve the following tricky conundrums:

> My first is equality.
> My second is inferiority.
> My whole is superiority.

> My first is a preposition.
> My second is a composition.
> My whole is an acquisition.

> My first is a thing for the feet.
> My second is long at the head.
> My whole is under the sheet
> Before anyone is in bed.

And the answers are: *peerless, fortune,* and *mattress.*

Everyone loves a charade. The most magical mystical charade words are those that fly open to yield other words that retain their spellings exactly and are related to the mother word:

ON A BEANSTALK, DO THE BEANS TALK?

YES!

*Many a new *adage* comes to us in an AD AGE.
**Alienation* characterizes A LIE NATION.
*We *atone* to be AT ONE with the universe.
*Poetry lovers are never *averse* to A VERSE.
*We try to *avoid* A VOID in our lives.
**Barflies* live in an atmosphere of BARF, LIES.
*A *barrage* of beer bottles often accompanies a BAR RAGE.
*On a *beanstalk,* do the BEANS TALK?
*Your adventures in *brokerage* could send you into a BROKE RAGE.
*When a metropolis is filled to *capacity,* it's time to CAP A CITY. Otherwise what mayor has the *mendacity* to claim he or she can MEND A CITY?

*A *caravan* often includes A CAR, A VAN.

*A *conspiracy* is a CONS' PIRACY.

*A *cutlass* can CUT LASS and lad.

*A *daredevil* DARED EVIL.

*Nations try *diplomatically* to acquire a DIPLOMATIC ALLY.

*A *generation* is a GENE RATION.

*To be *gentlemanly* is to be GENTLE, yet MANLY.

*Just as after a *gunshot,* the GUN'S HOT, being within *earshot* of gossip about you will make your EARS HOT.

*The *Heisman* trophy could be renamed the HE IS MAN trophy (or the IS HE MAN trophy).

*When we study *history,* we say, "HI, STORY!"

*If you *initiate* a trip to a restaurant, soon after you might exclaim,
  "IN IT I ATE!"
*Your *identity* is your I. D. ENTITY.
*Someone who has become *irate* about being neglected might shout,
  "I RATE!"
*An *island* IS LAND.
*An incompetent *mendicant* might exclaim, "MEND? I CAN'T!"
*A *novice* in a convent is likely to have NO VICE.
*An *onus* is ON US.
*When governments *overtax,* they use an OVERT AX on our wallets.
*Gail Sheehy's book *Passages* studies how we PASS AGES.
**Pungent* wit makes a PUN GENT.
*A *soap opera* makes us sigh, "SO, A POP ERA."
*An equestrian will *reinforce* a horse's good habits by applying the
  proper REIN FORCE.
*They think our hard-earned money is *theirs* because they are THE IRS.
*One might call out to *yeomen,* "YE, O MEN."

Some words can be charaded in more than one way. *Marshall,* for example, can appear as:

MAR SHALL   MARS HALL   MARSH ALL

Noyes is a common last name that can be divided into two opposites:
NO YES. *Mason* is another last name that can be oxymoronically cleft: MA
SON. Tucked into a *nook* are NO and OK.
  The Word Circus would never want to get supermathematical about let-
ter play. But, for fun only, we'll charade *supermathematical* from left to right:

SUP   ER   MAT   HE   MA   TI   CAL.

Then we'll charade from right to left to produce:

LAC   IT   AM   EH   TAM   RE   PUS.

Now, each of the seven words in the forward charade reverses each of the seven words in the semordnilapic charade:

SUP/PUS   ER/RE   MAT/TAM   HE/EH   MA/AM   TI/IT   CAL/LAC.

Among the rarest of letter patterns are semordnilapic charade words, in which words tumble out of the larger word, but in reverse order:

lonesome	ME SO LONE.	Galahad	HAD A GAL.
hideous	US O HIDE.	poetry	TRY POE.

More pyrotechnically, a *notable* doctor was NOT ABLE to operate because he had NO TABLE.

In *The Scarlet Letter,* Hester Prynne asked, "Must I add AN A TO MY *anatomy?*"

A *toreador* who had never learned TO READ OR write, when asked for his signature, gave this *significant* reply: "How can I SIGN IF I CAN'T write?"

If a boy and a girl are *amiable together,* he may well wonder, "AM I ABLE TO GET HER?"

Even longer sentences can be charaded into new statements, using the same letters in their very same sequence:

Version 1: HA! THOU TRAGEDY INGRATE, DWELL ON, SUPERB OLD STAG IN GLOOM.
Version 2: HATH OUTRAGE, DYING, RATED WELL? ON SUPER-BOLD STAGING LOOM!
Version 1: FLAMINGO: PALE, SCENTING A LATENT SHARK!
Version 2: FLAMING, OPALESCENT IN GALA TENTS — HARK!

In the anticharade, one word changes into a statement that means the opposite of the base word. *Cars kill* because of a lack of CAR SKILL:

amok	AM O.K.	searing sun lit island	SEA RINGS UNLIT ISLAND.
inaction	IN ACTION	seashell	SEA'S HELL
manslaughter	MAN'S LAUGHTER	therapist	THE RAPIST
nowhere	NOW HERE	warship	WAR'S HIP.

This palindromic charade sentence forms the first conversation ever spoken:

"MADAM, I'M ADAM."
"MAD AM I? MAD AM?"

Now step right up to some variations of charade words. Watch as we combine a loop-the-loop with a charade:

Start with the word *safari.* Move the back letter to the front, and then cleave the word. The result — IS AFAR.

Start with *waste,* and relocate the *w* to the end. Then charade, and you'll find that when we *waste* resources, we end up in a A STEW.

Is there a more spectacular feat in language than the looping and charading of *cabaret?* Move the *c* from the front to the back and — presto, chango! — you stand in the presence of:

A BAR, ETC.,
which is just what a cabaret is!

Like the frosty layers of a snowball, snowball words are made of words that increase by one letter at a time:

damage = d/am/age
fatherless = f/at/her/less
temperamentally = t/em/per/amen/tally

Reverse snowball words melt in your mittens, one letter at a time:

banana = ban/an/a
altogether = alto/get/he/r
plainclothesmen = plain/clot/he's/me/n

In alternades the hidden words are systematically built by using every other letter:

calliopes = clips + aloe
chainlets = canes + hilt
fleetness = fetes + lens
lounge = lug + one
schooled = shoe + cold
spouts = sot + pus
triennially = tinily + renal

Now we move up to trinades, in which three words hide, each formed by every third letter!:

> decorated = dot + ere + cad
> liberated = let + ire + bad
> moderated = met + ore + dad
> penitence = pin + etc. + nee
> separated = sat + ere + pad
> similarly = sir + ill + may
> tabulated = tut + ale + bad

Bookend words offer one more way to recombine all the letters in a word. Take an eight-letter word — say, *betrayer*. Then yoke together the first and last two letters to form a word — *beer* — leaving the middle four letters to form a second word — *tray*. *Beer tray*. Teetotalers and prohibitionists would contend that a beer tray can indeed be a betrayer.

The reconfiguration of *demeaned* into *mean deed* also makes good sense, as perhaps does *resident* into *side rent*.

Other eight-letter exhibits are not so meaningful, but nonetheless intriguing:

> designer = deer + sign
> diminish = mini + dish
> honestly = holy + nest
> ligament = lint + game
> pilaster = last + pier
> rebelled = reed + bell
> recently = rely + cent
> remittal = real + mitt
> sediment = sent + dime

DIMINISH

MINI DISH

One seven-letter bookend word conceals two animals:

debater = deer + bat

Literary ladies and readerly gentlemen! Bookish boys and precocious girls! We close our extraordinary exhibition of charade words with the most magically mysterious of all concealed messages in literature.

The most luminous of all biblical translations is the King James Version, the brainchild of James I, who fancied himself a scholar and theologian. The King decided to assure his immortality by sponsoring a new Bible worthy of the splendor of his kingdom. Three years of loving labor, 1608-1611, produced what John Livingston Lowes called "the noblest monument of English prose." Few readers would dissent from that verdict.

But some commentators have wondered why William Shakespeare was apparently not included among the fifty-four translators chosen. After all, Shakespeare had already written *Macbeth* in honor of King James (who also fancied himself an expert on witchcraft), and what better committee member could one ask for than the greatest poet of his age to work with the greatest collection of religious literature of all ages?

But an intriguing peculiarity in the King James Bible suggests that Shakespeare was not entirely absent from the monumental project. In 1610, the year of most intensive work on the translation, Shakespeare was forty-six years old. Armed with this clue, we turn to the forty-sixth psalm as it appears in the King James Bible. Count down to the forty-sixth word from the beginning and then count up to the forty-sixth word from the end, excluding the cadential *Selah:*

God is our refuge and strength, a very present help in trouble.
Therefore will not we fear, though the earth be removed,
  and though the mountains be carried into the midst of the sea;
Though the waters thereof roar and be troubled,
  though the mountains shake with the swelling thereof. Selah.
There is a river, the streams whereof shall make glad the city of God,
  the holy place of the tabernacle of the Most High.
God is in the midst of her; she shall not be moved:
God shall help her, and that right early.
The heathen raged, the kingdoms were moved:
  he uttered his voice, the earth melted.
The Lord of hosts is with us; the God of Jacob is our refuge. Selah.
Come, behold the works of the Lord,
  what desolations he hath made on earth;
He maketh wars to cease unto the end of the earth;
  he breaketh the bow, and cutteth the spear in sunder;
  he burneth the chariot in the fire.
Be still, and know that I am God:
I will be exalted among the heathen, I will be exalted in the earth.
The Lord of hosts is with us; the God of Jacob is our refuge. Selah.

If you counted accurately, your finger eventually lit upon the two words *shake* and *spear*. Shakespeare.

Now count down from the first word to the fourteenth, and the word *will* appears. If you then count up from the ending, *Selah,* to the thirty-second word, you land on the two words *I am.* 14+32 = 46, the age of the Bard at the time of the translating of the King James version.

Will I am shake spear. Whether or not William Shakespeare created the majesty of the forty-sixth psalm, he is in it. Whether the embedded and cha-raded *will I am shake spear* is a purposeful plant or the product of happy chance, the name of the world's most famous poet reposes cunningly in the text of the world's most famous translation.

Perhaps that is why one anagram of the name *William Shakespeare* is WE LIKE HIS PSALM AREA.

THE SHRINKING SP●TLIGHT

WEARY

WILLIE

ALONE

LONE

ONE

Many aficionados of circus life consider Emmett Kelly the greatest pantomime clown of all time. Kelly played Weary Willie, a hobo whose sorrowful expression never changed, a pathetic bumbler who came out the loser in every situation. Willie was clad in a baggy brown suit of infinite tatters, large and leaky shoes, and the most dilapidated of derbies.

In Kelly's most famous act, he would sweep up a spotlight. Trying to clean up the arena, Kelly would methodically set about sweeping the floor. Working his way to the middle of the stage, he would find a pool of light. Though it was obvious to the audience that the source was a distant spotlight, he tried to sweep the splash of brightness away.

As he swept from the outside inward, the ring of light grew smaller and smaller. Finally, it became but a dot that Kelly carefully whisked into a dustpan or under a canvas ground cloth.

Like Emmett Kelly, we can shrink words a little at a time. One way to reduce a word is by beheading it. We cut away its first letter, and still a word remains.

Someone once wrote,

THE FIRST TIME
X MAN USED A WORD
INSTEAD OF A SWORD,
THAT WAS THE
BEGINNING OF
CIVILIZATION.

A WORD

How true. That was also an
inadvertent example of a beheadment, the chopping off of the first letter
of a word to create a second word, as in *sword/word*.
The beheadment of a word often produces a surprising result — and without the grisly consequences of real-life decapitation. Thus, through a blood-
less evolution, *who, what, where,* and *when* become *ho, hat, here,* and *hen*.

When a first letter is lopped off, one or more internal vowel sounds may
change:

bone/one	devil/evil	pirate/irate
cache/ache	dragout/ragout	slaughter/laughter
climb/limb	height/eight	wallow/allow
close/lose	hover/over	whose/hose
coverage/overage	orange/range	women/omen

The longest common words that can be beheaded are the fifteen-letter basewords *emotionlessness, gastronomically,* and *treasonableness.*

An array of words can be beheaded and then beheaded again, as in *preach/reach/each, scowl/cowl/owl,* and *women/omen/men.*

Multiple beheadments became a popular pastime in the nineteenth century, as in these two riddle poems, the first from *Charades, Enigmas, and Riddles* (1862) and the second from *Frolics of the Sphinx* (1812):

What is pretty and useful in various ways,
 Though it tempts some poor mortals to shorten their days;
Take one letter from it, and then will appear
 What youngsters admire every day of the year!
Take two letters from it, and then, without doubt,
 You are what it is, if you don't find it out.

* * *

Composed of only five letters am I,
 And us'd to express a day that is dry,
Or bright and unclouded, not such as we find,
 When the fogs of November enervate mankind;
One letter remove, and you've often read o'er,
 This favorite play of a bard we adore,
And sympathiz'd much o'er the scenes of distress,
 Which on his old hero so heavily press,
And have lent, with compassion, all that which remains
 To the highly wrought grief of his magical strains,
When this little word three letters contains.

The answer to the first conundrum is *glass* and to the second, *clear.*

This verse-atility inspires the Word Circus to present in-versely a poem about a seven-letter word that can be successively beheaded down to a single letter:

Ladies and gentlemen!

A number of beheadments of a single letter generate no essential loss of meaning. Often the discarded letter is *s,* which seems to act as a kind of intensifier:

select/elect	smash/mash	spike/pike	squash/quash
slather/lather	smelt/melt	splash/plash	stumble/tumble

Beheadments of letters other than *s* also result in synonyms:

alive/live	avow/vow	dalliance/alliance	prattle/rattle
amassing/massing	brash/rash	especially/specially	preserve/reserve
arouse/rouse	brim/rim	grumble/rumble	ramble/amble
ashamed/shamed	clump/lump	ledge/edge	roust/oust

Alone and *upraise* can be doubly beheaded and still retain their essential meanings:

alone	lone	one
upraise	praise	raise

Some beheadments produce the opposite of their basewords:

bonus/onus
covert/overt
lawful/awful
neither/either
never/ever
none/one
preview/review
she/he
there/here
yours/ours

With a few rare beheadments, it is possible to double the number of syllables when a letter is lopped off the front. The basewords tend to end in *-ed*, as in:

dragged/ragged   drugged/rugged   paged/aged   snaked/naked   twinged/winged

But one base word that does not wag an *-ed* tail nonetheless doubles its syllables when it loses its head:

vague/ague

Consider the following statement:

SHOW THIS BOLD PRUSSIAN THAT PRAISES SLAUGHTER, SLAUGHTER BRINGS ROUT. TEACH THIS SLAUGHTER-LOVER HIS FALL NEARS.

Watch what happens when we behead each word and fiddle with the punctuation:

HOW HIS OLD RUSSIAN HAT RAISES LAUGHTER — LAUGHTER RINGS OUT! EACH, HIS LAUGHTER OVER, IS ALL EARS.

Some words can be multiply beheaded two letters at a time:

DELIBERATING

LIBERATING

BERATING

RATING

TING

Needless Needles

Now naturally follow curtailments — words in which the last letter or letters may be removed and still remain words. Among the most fascinating curtailments are those that produce a new word that is basically unrelated in meaning to the first word. Some involve the terminal *s:*

brass/bras	caress/cares	discuss/discus	hiss/his	needless/needles
bugless/bugles	deadliness/deadlines	handless/handles	is/I	possess/posses

With the loss of the terminal *s,* words such as *princess* and *ogress* turn into the plural of their male counterparts — *princes* and *ogres.*
Other transformations curtail different letters:

area/are	diverse/divers	honey/hone	rabbit/rabbi
badger/badge	first/firs	lather/lathe	shrivel/shrive
camel/came	heaven/heave	priest/pries	suite/suit
daisy/dais	honest/hones	quartz/quart	weary/wear

The longest word that isn't a plural and that can be singly curtailed is *bulleting/bulletin*.

Some words actually gain a syllable when their tails are removed:

boat/boa   brassiere/brassier   ration/ratio   vial/via

Here is a curtailment riddle in verse. Can you supply the answer?:

> It's found in the sea like pirate's loot.
>   Cut off its tail, and now it's a fruit.
> Cut off its tail once more and you read
>   The name of a vegetable small as a seed.

The answer is:

PEARL

PEAR

PEA

More spectacularly, let's successively curtail the eight-letter *pasterns* until only a single letter remains:

PASTERNS

PASTERN

PASTER

PASTE

PAST

PAS

PA

P

**CLAM
CLAMP**

The Word Circus is now proud to present a menagerie of hidden animals that run and swim and fly and crawl out of words subject to single-letter deletions. First, come beasts that emerge from single beheadments or curtailments. You're invited to *assess* the *asses, clamp* a *clam, crown* a *crow, feel* an *eel, rant* about an *ant, regret* an *egret, share* a *hare, steal* a *teal* and discover a *craven raven, deft eft, puffing puffin, sadder adder, shrewd shrew, stern tern,* and other hidden animals:

apex/ape
beard/bear
been/bee
board/boar
boast/boas
cram/ram
drat/rat
groan/roan
potter/otter
scat/cat
scow/cow
then/hen

BEAR
BEARD

Then march and romp animals that, with the vanishing of a single letter from the front or back, materialize from within *other* animals. The results are both bovine and ovine:

bass/ass	boar/boa	fox/ox
beagle/eagle	fowl/owl	wasp/asp

BEAGLE
EAGLE

ARF!
CHIRP!

Combining beheadment and curtailment can produce intriguing results:

> I am an odd figure.
> Behead me: I'm even.
> Curtail me: I'm twilight
> And maiden in Eden.

The answer is:

SEVEN

EVEN

EVE

Here's a more extended alternation between curtailment and beheadment:

ASHAMED

ASHAME

SHAME

SHAM

HAM

HA

A

A random pattern of curtailment and beheadment gives us:

SHEATHED

SHEATHE

SHEATH

HEATH

HEAT

EAT

AT

A

Now let's behead and curtail at the same time:

ECLIPSE	HEARTHS	FLOWERS	PIRATES	SHEATHE
CLIPS	EARTH	LOWER	IRATE	HEATH
LIP	ART	OWE	RAT	EAT
I	R	W	A	A

Here are two nine-letter words that can be deleted anywhere while keeping the order of the letters intact:

SPARKLING
SPARKING
SPARING
SPRING
SPRIG
PRIG
PIG
PI
I

STARTLING
STARTING
STARING
STRING
STING
SING
SIN
IN
I

STARTLING !

Finally, we present for your entertainment the longest common word that can be transdeleted. That is, from the twelve-letter *reactivation* we can pluck out any letter, one at a time, and then form successively smaller anagrams, until but a single letter remains:

```
                    REACTIVATION
                    RATIOCINATE
                    RECITATION
                    INTRICATE
                    INTERACT
                    TAINTER
                    ATTIRE
                    IRATE
                    RATE
                    ART
                    AT
                    A
```

An acrostic is not an angry insect ("a cross tick"), any more than an oxy-moron is a big dumb cow. Rather, an acrostic is a composition, usually a poem, in which the first letter of each line spells out a hidden word or message. Thus, acrostics are the most complete type of deletion as nothing remains but a single letter per line.

The most widely read acrostics occur in literature. Should you have any doubt that Lewis Carroll wrote *Alice's Adventures in Wonderland* specifically for Alice Pleasance Liddell, take a closer look at the acrostic poem that concludes *Through the Looking Glass:*

> A boat, beneath a sunny sky,
> Lingering onward dreamily,
> In an evening of July —
>
> Children three that nestle near,
> Eager eye and willing ear,
> Pleased a simple tale to hear —
>
> Long has paled that sunny sky:
> Echoes fade and memories die:
> Autumn frosts have slain July.

Still she haunts me, phantomwise,
Alice moving under skies,
Never seen by waking eyes.

Children yet, the tale to hear,
Eager eye and willing ear,
Lovingly still nestle near.

It's a Wonderland they lie,
Dreaming as the days go by,
Dreaming as the summers die:

Ever drifting down the stream —
Lingering in the golden gleam —
Life, what is it but a dream?

In William Shakespeare's *A Midsummer Night's Dream,* the following passage, spoken by Titania, spells out her own name with the initial letters of each line:

Thou shalt remain here, whether thou wilt or no,
I am a spirit of no common rate,
The summer still doth tend upon my state;
ANd I do love thee. Therefore go with me.
I'll give thee fairies to attend on thee;
And they shall fetch thee jewels from the deep . . . .

Such acrostics are truly *A + B the C of D* — "Above and Beyond the Call of Duty."

KANGAROO WORDS

Ladies and gentlemen! Boys and Girls! Wordsters of all ages! Our circus is no dog and pony show — and to prove it, please turn your attention to the hippodrome track engirding the sawdust rings.

Paraders of the Lost Aardvark

All of Solomon's processions
And Croesus' gold and Trump's possessions
Cannot rival half the pomp
Of animals that march and romp.

What soul among us does not thrill
To a fiery hoop and a lion's skill,
The chittering of a monkey's laugh,
The mottled grace of a slim giraffe?

Who can be deaf to the ponderous sound
Of pachyderms that shake the ground,
Leathery monarchs lifting high
Their trumpet trunks to canvas sky?

Who is so proud as not to feel
A secret awe before a seal
That keeps such slick and moist repose
Spinning a ball upon its nose?

Who can forget a mighty horse
Capering through its circle course?
Who is so old who fails to heed
A lady in pink on a milk-white steed?

Ladies and gentlemen! Round and round the hippodrome track walk and run and trot and creep and fly and
swim a tentful of animals that are hidden in ordinary,
everyday words. All you have to do is delete some letters
from a baseword and a concealed animal will suddenly
appear, with all the letters in its name preserved:

apple/ape
armaments/ram, rat, ant
arsenals/ass, seal
behead/bee
bleat/bat
blizzard/lizard
botany/boa
bottler/otter
brushing/bruin
callow/cow
caramel/camel
chariot/cat
claim/clam

cranberry/crab, crane
deter/deer
everywhere/ewe
gloat/goat
grandeur/gander
harried/hare
heroin/heron
hoping/hog
hyphenate/hyena
igneous/gnu
jaunty/jay
larynx/lynx
lotion/lion

mackinaw/macaw
prig/pig
rectangle/eagle
showboat/shoat, bat
smolder/mole
snacked/snake
startling/starling
steeped/steed
swain/swan
throbbing/robin
towel/owl
trigger/tiger
wetlands/eland

Even more remarkable are the names of animals, letters in perfect order, that are nestled within other animals when key letters are deleted:

antelope/ape
coyote/coot
crocodile/cod
crow/cow
dove/doe
hedgehog/dog
mongoose/moose
oryx/ox
scarab/crab
springbok/pig
weasel/eel
wolverines/wolves

Inside both a *rabbit* and an *orangutan* squeaks a *rat*. Inside a *beaver* live both a *bear* and a *bee;* a *marmoset* enfolds both a *marmot* and a *mare;* and a *chameleon* can change into both a *camel* and a *hen.* Most meaningfully of all, cooped up in a *chicken* you can find another *hen!*

All of this bestial letter play serves to introduce the zoological epicenter of today's show. Prepare to be hopping glad as at the end of the mighty menagerie, in bounds an outbreak of Outback — a troupe of cute-faced, tall-tailed, ab-original, deep-pocketed kangaroos.

Being a marsupial, a mother kangaroo carries her young in her pouch. Kangaroo words do the same thing: Within their letters they conceal a smaller version of themselves — a joey, which is what a kangaroo's offspring is called. The joey must be the same part of speech as the mother kangaroo, and its letters must appear in order.

The special challenge of kangaroo words is that the joey must be a synonym; it must have the same meaning as the fully grown word. A *plagiarist* is a kind of *liar.* On the job, your *supervisor* is your *superior,* one of the largest joeys in captivating captivity.

Ab-Original Words

Hop right up to those kangaroo words,
   Slyly concealing whiz-bangaroo words,
Accurate synonyms, *cute* and *acute,*
   Hidden *diminutive* words, so *minute.*

Lurking inside of *myself* you'll find *me.*
   Just as inside of *himself* you'll find *he.*
Feel your mind *blossom;* feel your mind *bloom:*
   Inside a *catacomb*'s buried a *tomb.*

Kangaroo words are *precocious* and *precious*
   Flourishing, lush words that truly refresh us.
We're *nourished;* they *nurse, elevate,* and *elate* us.
   We're so *satisfied* when their synonyms *sate* us.

Kangaroo words both *astound* us and *stun*.
They're so darned *secure* that we're *sure* to have fun!
With *charisma* and *charm*, they're a letter-play wonder.
They *dazzle* and *daze* with their treasures, down under.

We must *regulate* and *rule* over what makes a kangaroo word. The letters of the joey must not be entirely adjacent. Like a kangaroo novice, each joey word must take at least one hop through the letters of the mother word. Although we find a *story* in *history*, *art* in a *cartoon*, a *cave* in a *cavern*, and a *rim* in the *perimeter*, these are not true kangaroos because all the letters in each joey are adjacent.

Among the kangaroo words that yield the most *joviality* and *joy* are those that conceal multiple joeys. Let's now *perambulate, ramble*, and *amble* through an exhibit of this species. Open up a *container* and you get a *can* and a *tin*. When you have *feasted*, you *ate* and have *fed*. When you *deteriorate*, you *rot* and *die*. A *routine* is both *rote* and a *rut*. Brooding inside *loneliness* are *loss* and *oneness*.

A *chariot* is a *car* and a *cart*. A charitable *foundation* is both a *fund* and a *font*. Within the boundaries of a *municipality* reside *city* and *unity*, while a *community* includes *county* and *city*.

Now hop right up to three supreme multi-generational kangaroo words that truly work:

disclosure	expurgated	frangible
clue	purged	fragile
cue	pure	frail

Encourage is an especially beguiling kangaroo because it gives birth to the joey *urge* and its opposite, *enrage*. From the verb *feast* issue *eat* and its opposite, *fast*. These examples invite exploration of kangaroos that conceal their own opposites. For instance, simply remove the *id* from *intimidated* and the result will be *intimate:*

animosity/amity
appeal/appal
avoid/aid
brandish/banish
communicative/mute
courteous/curt
cremate/create
deify/defy
exclude/exude
exist/exit
freezing/freeing
friend/fiend
gullible/glib
inattentive/intent

injured/inured
oblivious/obvious
patriarch/pariah
pest/pet
prurient/pure
resign/reign
resist/rest
saintliness/sin
spurns/spurs
stray/stay
threat/treat
uh-huh/uh-uh
vainglorious/valorous
wonderful/woeful

Now cast your eyes upon a rare species that reverses the process of multiple joeys, one in which two or more kangaroos give birth to the same joey:

irritated   infuriated
            irate

postured   positioned
            posed

jollity   jocularity

      joy

playfulness   facetiousness

      fun

exhilaration   exultation

      elation

lighted   illuminated

      lit

observe   spectate

      see

joined   confederated

      one

nougat		neurotic
	nut	
purged		pasteurized
	pure	
unanimity		uniformity
	unity	
closemouthed		uncommunicative
	mute	
rampage		ravage
	rage	
Brobdignagian		lumbering
	big	
impair		malform
	mar	
latest		least
	last	
foundation		fountain
	font	
slippery	stealthy	slinky
	sly	
transgressions	perversions	misdoings
	sins	

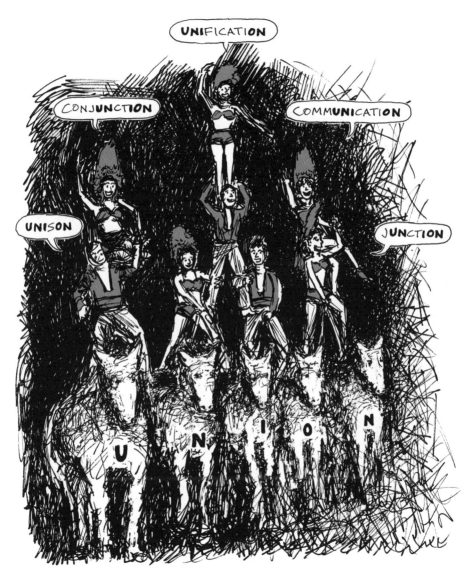

And now the spotlight falls on the two most multi-parented joeys in the circus!:

falsities   falsifies   fallacies   plagiarizes   reclines   calumnies   hyperbolizes
lies

deceased   departed   deactivated   decapitated   decayed   disintegrated   deteriorated   diseased
dead

But that's not all! It ain't over yet, folks! Just when you thought the act was over and the marsupial panorama completely presented and represented, into the *arena area* bound another company of kangaroo words! I guarantee that this final *burst* of aboriginality won't be a *bust*. I promise that this finale will prove not to be *superfluous,* but rather a *plus:*

MASCULINE

abstinence/absence
allegiance/alliance
appropriate/apt
barren/bare
barricaded/barred
because/as
brush/bush
chocolate/cocoa
christening/rite
coldhearted/hard
combination/coition
compadres/cadre
complemented/complete
contaminate/taint
controlled/cool
courtesy/curtsy
curtail/cut
damsel/dame

deliberated/debated
destruction/ruin
determine/deem
devilishly/evilly
disappointed/sad
discourteous/curt
displeasure/ire
disputation/spat
disseminated/sent
earlier/ere
entwined/tied
evacuate/vacate
evidenced/evinced
exhausted/used
exhortation/oration
exorcise/excise
facade/face
fairy/fay

fatigue/fag
flounder/founder
forbiddance/ban
fulminate/fume
healthier/haler
honorable/noble
hostelry/hotel
indolent/idle
inheritor/heir
instructor/tutor
investigate/vet
knapsack/pack
latest/last
lonely/only
masculine/male
matches/mates
misinterpret/err
moisture/mist
outspoken/open
palate/plate
perceivable/pale
petrochemical/oil
pinioned/pinned
playfellow/pal
precipitation/rain
prematurely/early
prosecute/sue
quiescent/quiet
rambunctious/raucous
rapscallion/rascal
recapitulate/relate
reduplicate/replicate
rendition/edition

respite/rest
restrain/rein
revived/revved
rotund/round
salvage/save
scholarship/cash
scion/son
separated/parted
shadowy/shady
slithered/slid
sparse/spare
splatter/spatter
splotch/spot

steamy/seamy
stricken/sick
strives/tries
struggled/tugged
tolerate/let
tosspot/sot
twitch/tic
unsightly/ugly
valedictorian/victor
variegated/varied
welded/wed
wriggle/wiggle
yearning/yen

Some kangaroos carry multiple words that form an expression closely related to the parent word. *Chocolate* is an ingredient in *hot cocoa*. When Moses *separated* the water, he *parted* the *Red Sea*. A *government* rules *over men*. It is but a short leap to make kangaroo-watching an exercise in social satire and editorial opinionizing:

WEIGHT WATCHERS ARE REFORMED EATERS.

*An *enthusiast* can easily become a *nut.*
*Your *passion* can become your *pain.*
*If you play slot machines advertised as *loose,* you will *lose* your money.
*Is the *Internal Revenue Service* fraught with *inner vice?*
*These days, *politicians* make us want to throw *pots* and *pans* at them. That's because *political promises* reveal themselves to be *piles* of *lies* and *pap* — merely *poll prose* and *poll poses.*
*To Democrats, *Republicans* are *relics* — mere *replicas* of nineteenth-century conservatism.
*People who attend a *Democrat picnic* make Republicans exclaim, *"Drat! Demonic!"*
*If you're seeking *discordance,* just go to a *disco dance.*
*Much *air pollution* is caused by the *auto.*
Weight watchers are reformed *eaters.*
Public relations can hide a bunch of *lies.*
*The *welfare system* is fraught with *waste.*
*Is *carjacking* on the increase because of *crack?*
Investigative reporters often *instigate negative* results.
*America's youth has got to be persuaded that *school* is *cool.*
*The *Internet* produces many an *intent* but *inert* hacker.
*It's an act of *compromising* when one ends up *composing* today's popular music and lyrics.
*Does the *Budweiser* Company really believe that it is *wiser* to drink *beer?*
*A *prosperous financier* is likely to have a *proper* and *fancier fiance* than we do. That's because people who are *affluent* with a *fortune* are bound to have *fun, fun.*

*Tensions in the Middle East have caused many a *Semite* to *smite* another.

*Inside the head of many a *wacko* are visions of *Waco.*

*The world has watched *Prince* Charles pay the *price* of being heir to one of the world's most famous *thrones* and go through the *throes* of a very public divorce.

*In the *expectorations* of Pavlov's dogs were great *expectations*. Indeed, the *salivation* of those dogs became the *salvation* of experimental psychology.

*If *imperialism* is a *peril,* is *democracy* in *decay?*

*How do we know that Russia is experiencing difficulty with its economy? Because the *ruble* is in *trouble.*

Ladies and gentlemen! Boys and girls! Children of all ages! Part of our fascination with kangaroo words is that all the letters of the joey appear in perfect order in the parent word. Hustle your bustle, now, to a letter-perfect parade of words whose order of letters astounds us and stuns us:

ARCHETYPICAL

Here we have the longest word with the most letters in alphabetical place. In *archetypical,* the letters *a, c, e, i,* and *l* are invariant. They occur as the first, third, fifth, ninth, and twelfth letters, just as they occur in the alphabet.

Ross Eckler has constructed an invariant sentence: "A bad egg hit KLM wipers two ways," in which *a, b, d, e, g, h, i, k, l, m, p, r, s, t, w,* and *y* all occupy their foreordained alphabetic slots.

BEGINS

A small community of six-letter words are composed of letters that appear in alphabetical order without repetition. Among them are *abhors, almost, begins, biopsy, chinos,* and *chintz.*

BILLOWY

The longest word (seven letters) whose letters are in alphabetical order, with one letter repeated. Matched only by *beefily.*

COUPON

Some of us pronounce this word as *kyu-pon,* others as *koo-pon.* With the first interpretation, *coupon* consists of four consecutive letters – QPON – in reverse order.

ELEMENT

In this elemental word we hark to the sound of three consecutive letters coming one after the other — LMN(t).

FACETIOUS

What did one of the poet Housman's debtors write to him? "A.E., IOU." The shortest (nine letters) and most accessible word that contains all five major vowels in sequence is *facetious.* AEIOU words that test the outré limits of the English language include *abstemious, abstentious, acheilous, acheirous, adventitious, aparecious, areious* (the shortest), *annelidous, arsenious, arterious, atenisodus, bacterious, caesious, fracedinous, lamelligomphus* (the longest), *lateriporous,* and *parecious.*

INOPERATIVE
The champion letter-order word for the second half of the alphabet, beginning with *n,* is *inoperative,* in which *n, o, p, r, t,* and *v* each repose in its proper alphabetic niche.

OVERSTUFFED
Along with *overstudious* and *understudy, overstuffed* is stuffed with four adjacent letters of the alphabet in order. Also worthy of mention is *analyzable,* which features the cluster *YZAB.*

Words containing five alphabetical letters in order but not adjacent are *absconded* and *ambuscade* — *ABCDE* — and *prizefighting* — *EFGHI.*

SPONGED
Tied with *wronged, sponged* is the longest word (seven letters) with all its letters in reverse alphabetical order, with no letters repeated.

SPOONFEED
The longest word (nine letters) with all its letters in reverse alphabetical order, with some letters repeated.

UNNOTICEABLY
The shortest English word (eleven letters) that contains the major vowels in reverse order, each occurring only once. Others include *subcontinental* and *uncomplimentary* (at fifteen letters the longest such word).

Ross Eckler crafted the sentence "Unsociable housemaid discourages facetious behaviour" to illustrate the point that the major vowels can occur, exactly once, in just about any order.

UNSOCIABLE HOUSEMAID
DISCOURAGES FACETIOUS BEHAVIOUR

THE ACROBAT

The flying trapeze was invented in 1859 by a Frenchman named Jules Leotard. The flying trapeze doesn't fly, of course; it is the acrobats who fly. The catcher on the shorter trapeze kicks hard and lets his body slip down until his legs wrap around the trapeze. He reaches out his arms.

Across the high tent, up on a high platform, the other flyers watch the catcher's rhythms closely. At exactly the right moment, one flyer grasps the trapeze, jumps up high, and swings out hard — beyond the realm of ordinary lives.

The drum rolls.

On the second swing out, the trapeze artist lets go of the bar and catapults high into the air, end over end. For one thrilling moment he soars to the very top of the tent. At the last second, the airy athlete reaches out and locks perfectly in the waiting grasp of the catcher.

Thrill-seeking children of all ages! High above the sawdust stage you are about to gaze upon words that fly through the air and change from one form to another along the way. Absolutely no flash photography, please!

In *London Society* (1867), the author of the following poem called the letters of the hidden words "feet." What are the two words the poet had in mind?:

> On six feet, I am a noxious drink,
>   Of whose effects you shudder to think.
> Change only my second foot, and then
>   You convert me into a horrible den
> Where the culprit, who gave the noxious drink,
>   Awaits the fate of which you shudder to think.

The answers are *poison/prison.* The change of a single letter causes a dramatic shift in meaning.

Can you change the first letter in a word that means "suspecting something wrong" to produce another word that means "boding something favorable"?

The answers are *suspicious/auspicious.*

Can you change an internal letter in a word that means "a significant moment" to produce another word that means "a heavy burden"?

The answers are *milestone* and *millstone.*

Can you change one letter in the name of a Middle Eastern country to generate the name of another Middle Eastern country? Can you do the same thing with two European countries?

The answers are *Iran/Iraq* and *Ireland/Iceland* (and yes, Iceland is a European country).

Now let's watch as one Word Circus animal transforms itself into another, then another, and yet another, and then performs the trick all over again:

> I fly like a baseball, a wing'd heavy hitter.
>   Change my first letter; I'm the pick of the litter.
> Do it again; I'm a rodent — no flattery.
>   Now change my last, and you'll charge me with battery.

* * *

> I start as an insect. Now change my first letter.
>   Now I'm a rodent. Please make me one better.
> Now change my middle. You've made me quite horny.
>   Now change my first. I love food that's corny.

The bestial solutions are: *bat/cat/rat/ram* and *louse/mouse/moose/goose*.

A bat and a louse and a moose are not the only animals that can be transformed into other animals by the substitution of a first letter:

beaver/weaver	donkey/monkey	hare/mare
dog/hog	guppy/puppy	seal/teal

And a rat and a mouse are not the only animals that become other animals with the change of a middle or terminal letter:

bear/boar	cod/cow	foal/fowl	lion/loon/coon/coot/colt

Now that you're familiar with the fun of substituting first letters, let's look at some word records. The only four-letter word that can yield thirteen new words by adding a letter at the front (if we count *qu-* as a single unit) is *ills* — *bills, dills, fills, gills, hills, kills, mills, pills, quills, rills, sills, tills,* and *wills. Ears* generates twelve new words by adding an initial letter — *bears, dears, fears, gears, hears, nears, pears, rears, sears, tears, wears,* and *years.* For a dozen variations on a six-letter word, look to *ailing* (again counting *qu-* as a single unit) — *bailing, failing, hailing, jailing, mailing, nailing, pailing, quailing, railing, sailing, tailing,* and *wailing.*

Two two-letter words — *at* and *ad* — can generate thirteen new words when one letter is added at the start — *at: bat, cat, eat, fat, gat, hat, mat, oat, pat, rat, sat, tat,* and *vat* and (again with *qu-* as a single unit) *ad: bad, cad, dad, fad, gad, had, lad, mad, pad, quad, sad, tad,* and *wad.*

For centuries, Word Circus aficionados have enjoyed creating vowel movements in order to change one word into another:

> A flea and a fly in a flue
> Were imprisoned, so what could they do?
> Said the flea, "Let us fly."
> Said the fly, "Let us flee."
> So they flew through a flaw in the flue.

This compact gimerick about the flea and the fly suggests a challenge: How many words can we turn into other words by inserting each of the five major vowels? Lest you think this is just a bunch of pap, let's start with *pap* itself. Not only is *pap* a palindrome, but it can transmogrify into seven different words by changing the internal vowel — *pap, peep, pep, pip, poop, pop,* and *pup* (to which we may add — phonetically, if not palindromically — *pipe* and *pope*).

We now present an array of other one-syllable words that run the gamut of each major vowel:

bad	bed	bid	bod	bud
bag	beg	big	bog	bug
ball	bell	bill	boll	bull
band	bend	bind	bond	bund

THE ILL VENDOR

last	lest	list	lost	lust
mad	med	mid	mod	mud
mash	mesh	mish-mosh		mush
mass	mess	miss	moss	muss
mate	mete	mite	mote	mute
pack	peck	pick	pock	puck
pall	pell mell	pill	poll	pull
pat	pet	pit	pot	put
tan	ten	tin	ton	tun

Now we'll move up a syllable and listen to the jangle of a nursery jingle:

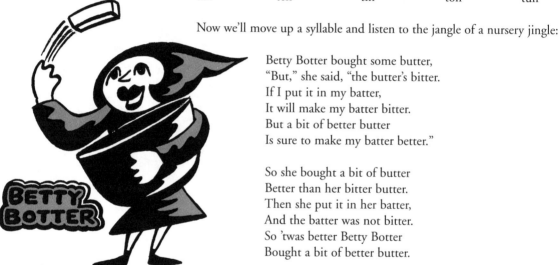

Betty Botter bought some butter,
"But," she said, "the butter's bitter.
If I put it in my batter,
It will make my batter bitter.
But a bit of better butter
Is sure to make my batter better."

So she bought a bit of butter
Better than her bitter butter.
Then she put it in her batter,
And the batter was not bitter.
So 'twas better Betty Botter
Bought a bit of better butter.

Botter, of course, is not a word, but the rhyme suggests the challenge of finding a two-syllable pattern that can integrate all five major vowels, one at a time. Four sequences fill the bill:

blander	blender	blinder	blonder	blunder
patted	petted	pitted	potted	putted
patter	petter	pitter-patter	potter	putter
patting	petting	pitting	potting	putting

148 • the acro bat

It's even more fun to change every letter of a word to create another word. The star of our word-into-word show is the acronimble, paranomazing Acro Bat. Watch now as the daring young Bat on the flying trapeze ascends the word ladder on the way to its death-defying, breath-denying performance.

Charles Lutwidge Dodgson, better known as Lewis Carroll, invented a new word game. The object is to change one letter at each step, while keeping the other letters in the same order, transforming that word into another word, often the opposite of the original. Each rung in the ladder must be a word in its own right. In the March 29, 1879, issue of *Vanity Fair,* he gave to the world a word game that he called doublets but that is now best known as word ladders. Gape as the Acro Bat ascends the ladder, begins with one word, and ends up at the opposite or contrasting word:

HEAD	HATE	APE	ARMY	BLACK	FLOUR
heal	rate	are	arms	blank	floor
teal	rave	ere	aims	blink	flood
tell	cave	err	dims	clink	blood
tall	cove	ear	dams	chink	brood
TAIL	LOVE	mar	dame	chine	broad
		MAN	name	whine	BREAD
			nave	WHITE	
			NAVY		

In Stanley Kubrick's brilliant film, *2001: A Space Odyssey*, the quirky, neurotic computer that runs the spaceship is named HAL. Each letter in *HAL* raised to the next letter turns out to be *I.B.M.* The *HAL*-to-*I.B.M.* transformation is an example of a shiftword pair. Certain words can be translated into other words by shifting each letter the same number of steps along the alphabet: from *adds* + 1 = *beet* to *balk* + 13 = *onyx*.

Joining the Acro Bat at the Word Circus are the *cold frog*, the *curl wolf*, the *sleep bunny*, the *papa dodo*, the *tuffet steeds*, the *harry bulls*, the *semi-cows*, the *owl god*, and the *pecan tiger*.

Let's illustrate five of these examples:

COLD	PECAN	BULLS	SLEEP	SEMI
dpme	qfdbo	cvmmt	tmffq	tfnj
eqnf	rgecp	dwnnu	unggr	ugok
FROG	shfdq	exoov	vohhs	vhpl
	TIGER	fyppw	wpiit	wiqm
		gzqqx	xqjju	xjrn
		HARRY	yrkkv	ykso
			zsllw	zltp
			atmmx	amuq
			BUNNY	bnvr
				COWS

PECAN
TIGER

Some shiftwords provide us with double plays and triple shiftwords:

ark + 3 = dun/dun + 14 = rib	fur + 6 = lax/lax + 7 = she
cot + 14 = oaf/oaf + 8 = win	law + 4 = pea/pea + 4 = tie
elm + 3 = hop/hop + 12 = tab	log + 6 = rum/rum + 2 = two

Animals prowl the forest of triple shiftwords:

add + 1 = bee/bee + 7 = ill	bus + 6 = hay/hay + 8 = pig
ant + 11 = lye/lye + 2 = nag	dodo + 6 = juju/juju + 6 = papa
ape + 11 = lap/lap + 4 = pet	irk + 9 = rat/rat + 4 = vex

No surprise that God would be involved in the grandest of all shiftgram clusters — a quadruple shiftword, involving yet another animal:

god +8 = owl   owl +4 = sap   sap +4 = wet   wet + 10 = god!

A number of shiftgrams are rather evocative:

bomb + 6 = hush	ice + 2 = keg
cubed + 10 = melon	lawn + 4 = pear
end + 1 = foe	oafs + 6 = ugly
etch + 12 = pens	open + 4 = stir
fang + 4 = jerk	wheel + 7 = dolls

Among four-letter shiftgrams, *gnat* +13 = *tang* is remarkable because *gnat tang* makes a kind of sense (at least if you're an insect-eater) and is also a palindrome.

The longest shift-pairs using reasonably common English words are composed of six letters:

fusion +6 = layout	manful + 7 = thumbs
muumuu + 10 = weewee	steeds + 1 = tuffet

and seven-letters:

abjurer +13 = nowhere   primero + 3 = sulphur

As always, the most satisfying transformations involve the emergence of a synonym or near synonym:

irk + 13 = vex   inkier + 7 = purple
cheer + 7 = jolly   oui + 10 = yes
green + 13 = terra   USA + 12 = gem!

Now we exhibit yet another way that words fly through space from trapeze to trapeze to become other words. Pig Latin is an oral language code that many children learn. It works by moving the initial consonant of a word to the end of it and adding *ay*. If the word begins with a vowel sound, *ay* is added to the end without changing anything else.

Ladies and gentlemen! The Acro Bat will now swoop from an array of English words to their pig Latin equivalents that are also real words or phrases. In doing so, the Bat will travel a *true route,* both of those words yielding the strange adjective *outré*.

beast/east bay   rex/x-ray
devil/evil day   sass/assay
lout/outlay   slice/ice sleigh
lover/overlay   stout/outstay
plover/overplay   trice/ice tray
plunder/underplay   wonder/underway

And, most spectacularly, what do you empty into your trash?:

trash/ashtray!

To write prose is human, to write poetry porcine. The pig Latin for *poem* suggests that poets should receive money for their work — poem = *Owe 'em? Pay!* Nevertheless, the Word Circus offers the following poem, free of charge and worth every penny!

True But Outré

As I was walking on the beach,
    Each bay
Was sunny, and I tried to reach
    Each ray.

I found some gold. I thought that more
    Ore may
Be hidden. In the ancient lore,
    Ore lay

On islands where the farmers hold
    Old hay
In caves that wind around the bold
    Old bay.

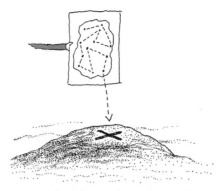

A map had shown the ancients wits
    Its way
To treasures buried in the pits:
    Its pay

BONK!
WHAM!
CRASH!
BUZZ!
POW!
BOING!

Was large enough to fill a bin
    In bay.
By silent night, or by the din
    In day,

I vowed that I would search the sand
    And say
That I would find the golden land
    And lay

Within the cave. I'd cook some meat,
    Eat. May
The horses join me in the heat,
    Eat hay,

And gallop to the ocean's spring-
    Ing spray,
Until I see my fortune's ring-
    Ing ray.

With luck I'll find the places
    Aces play
A lucky hand. I take ten paces.
    Aces pay.

Ladies and gentlemen! Boys and girls! For our closing act of soaring from word to word we shall gag you with a spoonerism!

The Reverend William Archibald Spooner entered the earthly stage near London on July 22, 1844, born with a silver spoonerism in his mouth. He set out to be a bird watcher but ended up instead as a word botcher. As the legend proclaims, he tended to reverse letters and syllables to produce many tips of the slung. For example, he once supposedly lifted a tankard in honor of Queen Victoria. As he toasted the reigning monarch, he exclaimed, "Three cheers for our queer old dean!"

That was appropriate because Dr. Spooner became a distinguished master and warden at Oxford University. But because of his frequent tips of the slung, he became famous for his tonorous rubble with tin sax. In fact, these switcheroos have become known as spoonerisms.

The larger the number of words in a language, the greater the likelihood that two or more words will rhyme. Because English possesses almost four times the number of words of any other language, it is afflicted with a delightful case of rhymatic fever. A ghost town becomes a toast gown. A toll booth becomes a bowl tooth. A bartender becomes a tar bender. And your local Wal-Mart becomes a Mall Wart!

More rhymes mean more possible spoonerisms. That's why English is the most tough and rumble language, full of thud and blunder. That's why English is the most spoonerizable tongue ever invented. That's why you will enter this tent optimistically and leave it misty optically.

All the spoonerisms in the Word Circus have points to them — so they're really forkerisms, especially this spoonerhyme:

Ladies and gentlemen! Gadies and lentlemen! Movers and shakers! Shovers and makers! In honor of Dr. William Archibald Spooner's tang tongueled whiz and witdom, we present a gallimaufry of tinglish errors and English terrors:

Dr. Spooner's Animal Act

Welcome, ladies; welcome gents.
   Here's an act that's so in tents:
An absolute sure-fire parade,
   A positive pure-fire charade —
With animals weak and animals mild,
   Creatures meek and creatures wild,
With animals all in a row.
   We hope that you enjoy the show:

Gallops forth a curried horse,
   Trotting through a hurried course.
Ridden by a loving shepherd
   Trying to tame a shoving leopard.
Don't think I'm a punny phony,
   But next in line's a funny pony.
On its back a leaping wizard,
   Dancing with a weeping lizard.

Watch how that same speeding rider
   Holds aloft a reading spider.
Now you see a butterfly
   Bright and nimbly flutter by,
Followed by a dragonfly,
   As it drains its flagon dry.
Step right up; see this mere bug
   Drain the drink from his beer mug.

Lumbers forth a honey bear,
  Fur as soft as bunny hair.
Gaze upon that churning bear,
  Standing on a burning chair.
Gently patting a mute kitten,
  In each paw a knitted mitten.
Watch as that small, running cat
  Pounces on a cunning rat.

See a clever, heeding rabbit
  Who's acquired a reading habit,
Sitting on his money bags,
  Reading many bunny mags,
Which tickle hard his funny bone,
  As he talks on his bunny phone.
He is such a funny beast,
  Gobbling down his bunny feast

Gasp in awe as winking seals
  Sit atop three sinking wheels.
Don't vacillate. An ocelot
  Will oscillate a vase a lot.
There's a clever dangling monkey
  And a stubborn, mangling donkey
And — a gift from our Dame Luck —
  There waddles in a large lame duck.

That's Dr. Spooner's circus show,
    With animals all in a row.
(As you can see, we give free reign
    To this metrical refrain.)
Now hops a dilly of a frog
    Followed by a frilly dog.
Hear that hoppy frog advise:
    "Time's fun when you're having flies!"

DAME LUCK

That's a look at spoonerisms in one swell foop. Now, before you move on to the next act, I offer you a special toast. Here's champagne to our real friends — and real pain to our sham friends!

Way up high, at the very top of the Big Top, more than a hundred feet above the ring, a metal cable less than an inch wide stretches between two tall towers. This is the altitudinous world of the high wire, or tightrope.

Swaying precariously onto the rope ventures the wire walker — a miracle of balance, a defiance of danger. Perilously above the crowd, the walker dances across the airy stretch and treads on space. The band plays a slow waltz, then the drum rolls while thousands of eyes watch.

Some tightrope walkers use a long pole to help them balance. Our wire-walking words use nothing but the beauty and economy of their forms as they dance and even jump rope along a bridge of thread in the air high above the crowd. Along the ineffable line between language and fantasy they frolic weightlessly on thin air.

First onto the wire is a cluster of one-syllable words that — believe it or not; and you soon will believe it! — do not include any of the major vowels, *a, e, i, o,* or *u!* That's right, ladies and gentlemen and boys and girls. You won't find any *ladies* or *gentlemen* or *boys* or *girls* in this lexicon. In this game you just can't buy a vowel.

WORDS ON A WIRE

With tongue firmly planted in cheek, some call these vowelless words "abstemious" words, a facetious label since *abstemious* (along with *facetious*) is fraught with every major vowel, and in sequence.

How many words missing any major vowel are there? Pay your money, and we'll introduce you to more than fifty — even as we exclude bizarre specimens such as *cwm, qyrqhyz,* and *crwth.*

Among these familiar abstemious words are *by, cry, cyst(s), dry, fly, fry, glyph(s), gym(s), gyp(s), hymn(s), lymph(s), lynch, lynx, my, nymph(s), ply, pry, shy, sky, sly, spry, spy, sty, sylph(s), synch(s), thy, try, why(s),* and *wry.*

Add two letters to *cry,* and you get *crypt.*

Add two letters to *try,* and still avoid using any major vowels in *tryst.*

Add two letters to *my,* and you get *myth;* add three and you get *myrrh.*

Among two-syllable words that exclude *a, e, i, o,* and *u* are *gypsy, pygmy, flyby,* and the abverbs *dryly, shyly, slyly, spryly,* and *wryly.* Each of these possesses two *y*'s, but one common two-syllable word of this type includes only one *y.*

The word is *rhythm(s).*

One three-syllable word also avoids the major vowels — *syzygy,* which means "the nearly straight-line configuration of three celestial bodies." *Syzygy* is an especially appropriate spelling for such a heavenly three-syllable word.

A Sonnet to Abstemious Words

Once did a *shy* but *spry gypsy*
Spy a *pygmy,* who made him feel tipsy.
Her form, like a *lynx, sylph,* and *nymph,*
Made all his *dry* glands feel quite *lymph.*

He felt so in *synch* with her *rhythm*
That he hoped she'd *fly* to the *sky* with him.
No *sly myth* would he *try* on her;
Preferring to *ply* her with *myrrh*.

When apart, he would *fry* and then *cry,*
Grow a *cyst* and a *sty* in his eye.
That's *why* they would *tryst* at the *gym,*
By a *crypt*, where he'd write a *wry hymn*.

Her he loved to the *nth* degree,
Like a heavenly *syzygy.*

Now that you're wise to the *y*'s, ask yourself if any words cavort across the wire without any *a, e, i, o,* or *u* — or the minor vowels *y* or *w.*

Hmm . . . That's one that you can find in some dictionaries, including Scrabble lexicons. We're not including abbreviations, such as *TV* and *Ph.D.*

Shh . . . Before you grab some *z*'s, give us some time to think. There, you've just spotted another two, along with *brr, pfft,* and *tsk-tsk.*

We sincerely hope that these abstemious words have pleased you, not just to the first, fifth, or tenth degree, but (and embedded in the poem above) to the *nth* degree!

Now onto the tightrope venture mirror words. To reflect on what a mirror word is and capitalize on the tricks that they play in a looking glass, please hold the next line up to the nearest mirror:

A B C D E F G H I J K L M N O P Q R S T U V W X Y Z

The letters that possess vertical symmetry — meaning that their left and right sides are mirror images of each other — are *A, H, I, M, O, T, U, V, W, X,* and *Y.* These eleven letters individually appear the same in a mirror as they do on a page. In a sense, each letter is a self-contained palindrome. Ross Eckler put these letters together to make a single expression, IVY MOUTH WAX, the brand name of a fictitious toothpaste.

The longest words spelled entirely with letters of vertical symmetry are MOUTH-TO-MOUTH and HOITY-TOITY.

B, C, D, E, H, I, K, O, and *X* have horizontal symmetry in common: Their top halves and bottom halves reflect each other. As a result, these letters reflect perfectly in a mirror when they are flipped on their heads. They're all in the sentence HECK, I'D BOX.

The longest word (nine letters) made from horizontally symmetrical letters is the nine-letter CHECKBOOK. Runners up include CHECKED, COOKBOOK, DECIDED, DECODED, and EXCEEDED.

"Echo," the horizontally symmetrical poem you're about to read, appears with its title and lines in reverse order. Simply turn the page upside down and hold the text up to the mirror:

DIED.
ED CHOKED,
HOODED IBEX.
DECIDED DICED DODO,
COOKBOOK —
DEBBIE COOKED
CODEBOOK.
BOB CODED
CHECKBOOK.
DEEDEE CHECKED
  ECHO

Only four letters — *H, I, O,* and *X* — are symmetrical along both axes, meaning that they appear the same in a mirror as they do on a page — even when they are turned upside down. You might greet these letters in alphabetical order: HI, OX!

Morton Mitchell constructed a palindrome of fearful symmetry — TOO HOT TO HOOT. Note that, as well as consisting entirely of vertically self-reflective letters, this palindrome is univocalic (one vowel only).

Taking off from Mitchell's hoot of a palindromic statement, George Marvell has crafted a univocalic, vertically symmetrical palindromic conversation, between or among owls:

"TOO HOT TO HOOT!"
"TOO HOT TO WOO!"
"TOO WOT?"
"TOO HOT TO HOOT!"
"TO WOO!"
"TOO WOT?"
"TO HOOT! TOO HOT TO HOOT!"

Next marches in a reflective parody of Henry Wadsworth Longfellow's "Hiawatha." In "AHTAWAIH," each character is letter-perfect but word-crazy. To get to the shores of Gitchie Gumee, you'll need to hold the poem up to the mirror:

OTTO TUOHTIW OTUA TAHT HTIW
IIAWAH TA AHTAWAIH
— !IXAT A TAHW — IXAT A TIH
.IMAIM TA ATOYOT A

:YVI OT WOV I TUH A TA
.IXAT A TIH AHTAWAIH”
HATU OT TUO TI WOT YAM I
“!YXAW OOT — WOT OT TIAW YAM I

IXAT A HTIW OTTO TUOHTIW
IIAWAH TA AHTAWAIH
-IXAM A — AMIXAM A TIH
!IMAIM TA (OTUA YM) AM

:AVA HTIW TUH A TA MA I
.OTUA YM TIH AHTAWAIH”
.ITIHAT OT TI WOT YAM I
“.OTTO OT TOOT OT TIAW YAM I

AHTAWAIH HTIW YOT YAM I
.OIHO — AWOI TA TUO
IXAT HTOMMAM TAHT WOT YAM I
.UHAO OT — IIAWAH OT

Next out onto the almost-invisible rope are the flying pangrams. Many typists know *The quick brown fox jumps over a lazy dog* as a thirty-three-letter sentence that employs every letter in the alphabet at least once. Such sentences are called pangrams.

Look up at the canvas heavens and fix your eyes on a sampling of the best pangrams of even fewer letters. What you are about to see are meaningful sentences that avoid obscure words yet contain every letter of the alphabet:

Pack my box with five dozen liquor jugs. (thirty-two letters)
Jackdaws love my big sphinx of quartz. (thirty-one)
How quickly daft jumping zebras vex. (thirty)
Quick wafting zephyrs vex bold Jim. (twenty-nine)
Waltz, nymph, for quick jigs vex Bud. (twenty-eight)
Bawds jog, flick quartz, vex nymph. (twenty-seven)

HOW QUICKLY DAFT
JUMPING ZEBRAS VEX.

And now, ladies and gentlemen, the Peter Pangram of all pangrams —

Mr. Jock, TV quiz Ph.D., bags few lynx. (twenty-six!)

If you can come up with a twenty-six letter pangram that makes easy sense and does not resort to names, initials, or mutant words, rush it to the Word Circus and we'll make you famous.

Esteemed members of the Word Circus audience! Keep your eyes peeled and ears open as a troupe of words on a wire trips across the thin line that holds the quivering letters — and our attention. Each of the words you are about to see is crafted from a restricted set of letters (as with abstemious and mirror words) or is formed from a demandingly elegant pattern (as with pangrams):

AREA

A rare four-letter word crammed with three syllables. Among lower-case examples are *aria, idea, iota, oleo,* and *olio. Oreo, Iowa, Iona, Oahu,* and *Ohio* are capitalized specimens.

The shortest two-syllable words are the rather obscure *ai,* a three-toed sloth; *aa,* a rough lava; and *Io,* a moon of Jupiter.

ASSESSES

The longest word (eight letters) with one, and only one, consonant repeated throughout.

BOOKKEEPER

The only common word that features three consecutive pairs of double letters. It is easy to imagine the bookkeeper's assistant, a *subbookkeeper,* who boasts four consecutive pairs of double letters.

Now let's take a science-fantasy leap into language and conjure up a zoologist who helps maintain raccoon habitats. We'd call that zoologist a *raccoon nook keeper* — six consecutive sets of double letters! Now let's imagine another zoologist who studies the liquid secreted by chickadee eggs. We'd call this scientist a *chickadee egg goo-oologist* — and into the world is born three consecutive sets of triple letters!

Sweet-toothed is a hyphenated example of a word containing three adjacent double letters.

BAREFACED FEEDBACK

BRIGHT-FACED

Although *bright-faced* is not enshrined in any major dictionary, it is a plausible coinage. This shining compound embraces the first nine letters of the alphabet. Incredibly, nine of the eleven letters in *bright-faced* are part of the *a*-through-*i* letter string.

Words that feature six alphabetical letters, neither adjacent nor in order, are:

ABCDEF: backfield, barefaced, black-faced, feedback
DEFGHI: farsighted, figurehead, frightened, tightfisted
KLMNOP: kleptomania, phantomlike
QRSTUV: ventriloquist
PQRSTU: prerequisite, picturesque, quipsters
RSTUVW: liverwurst

In the list above, *black-faced* and *barefaced* boast the highest ratio of alphabetic letters (nine to one and eight to one).

Recognizably deserves recognition for its cyclical string of five alphabetic letters — *YZABC* — while *Kilimanjaro* stands tall for its seven-letter string — *IJKLMNO*. *Propinquities* ravels out the eight-letter string *NOPQRSTU*.

Now try this riddle: What common substance is represented by the eight-letter string *HIJKLMNO?* The answer (chuckle chuckle) is water. Get it? H to O.

CABBAGE

Lewis Carroll once wrote to a little girl: "With the first seven letters of the alphabet, I can make a word." That word was *big-faced (ABCDEFG* with an *I).* Clever, clever, but *big-faced* has questionable status as a word.

The more familiar *cabbage* is one of a number of seven-letter piano words, ones that can be spelled out using the musical notes ABCDEFG. Other seven-letter examples are *acceded, baggage, defaced,* and *effaced.* The ten-letter *cabbage-bed,* listed in at least one dictionary, is a tempting possibility.

Cabbage-headed (thirteen letters), meaning "stupid," has been suggested as the longest recognizable word cobbled entirely from letters in the first half of the alphabet. Other thirteen-letter candidates include the reduplications *diddle-daddled* and *fiddle-faddled.*

CATCHPHRASE

The most frequently used English word containing six consonants in a row, an internal pattern that also marks *latchstring, weltschmerz,* and *Knightsbridge,* a district in London.

CHTHONIC

Among the handful of words that begin with four consonants, most are of German or Yiddish origin and begin with *sch* — *schlemiel, schlep, schlimazel, schlock, schlump, schmaltz, schmatte, schmear, schmo, schmooze, schmutz, schnapps, schnauzer, schnitzel, schtick,* and *schwa.*

Quadri-consonantal words that begin with letters other than *s* include some of the most tongue-tangling, ear-rinsing specimens in our language — *chthonic* (relating to the spirits of the underworld), *phthisis* (tuberculosis), and *pschent* (an Egyptian double crown).

CIVIC

It's not just a palindrome, but, along with *civil, livid, mimic,* and *vivid,* the longest word (five letters) composed entirely of Roman numerals. If we assign each letter its Roman numerical value, *mimic* yields the highest total — 2,102 — and *civil* the lowest — 157.

COCKAMAMIE

The odd letters of our alphabet — *ACEGIKMOQSUWY* — include all the major vowels, along with *y.* We're not being cockamamie when we say that the longest, unaffixed word that can be cobbled from such odd letters is the ten-letter *cockamamie.*

Bereft of the major vowels, the longest words composed of even letters are *nth* and the sound-effect words *brr* and *pfft.*

COMMITTEE

The best known word with three double letters interrupted by one extraneous letter. Other members of this duplistic family include *assessee, coffee-room, keenness, Kissimmee, Tennessee,* and *yellowwood.*

DEEDED

The longest word consisting of two letters each used three times. *Deeded* can be typed with just one finger, along with *ceded, mummy, muumuu,* and *yummy.*

DEFENSELESSNESS

The longest univocalic word (fifteen letters), *defenselessness* has only one vowel, an *e* that occurs five times. *Senselessness* (thirteen letters) is the longest univocalic word that consists of but four different letters.

EERIE

The most common example among five-letter words with just one consonant. Another is *audio,* with five letters, four vowels, and three syllables. Then there's *Ouija* — the name of a board for divination that is still used for fun and fraud. *Ouija* is a conjunction of *yes* in French and German.

erroneousness

The letters *acemnorsuvwz* are called short letters because when set in lowercase type or written in cursive they do not poke their heads or feet above or below the line.

ERRONEOUSNESS IS THE LONGEST WORD (THIRTEEN LETTERS) CONSISTING ENTIRELY OF SHORT LETTERS,

THOUGH ONE COULD MAKE AN ARGUMENT FOR THE FIFTEEN-LETTER **OVERNERVOUSNESS.**

FILTH

This *tic-tac-toe tactic* is offered by our very own illustrious illustrator, Dave Morice, a *reward* of a *draw-er.* Note the tic-tac-toe grid below and ask yourself what letters can be traced along its lines. The letters, composed of straight, non-diagonal lines, are, alphabetically, *F, H, I, L,* and *T.* Each letter is a well-formed capital of the same height. With but the switch of a single letter, the five tic-tac-toe characters configure into FILTH. If you rotate the tic-tac-toe board forty-five degrees, you'll see that it has 4 X's. O, O, O, O those XXXX-rated words!

hijinks

The only common word that sports three consecutive lower-case dotted letters. *Beijing* and *Fiji* are the two most famous place-names that share this dotty letter pattern. Less renowned is Lake *Mijijie,* in Australia, which includes a five-dotted embedded palindrome.

HOTSHOTS

A number of words contain two adjacent sets of the same three letters. These are sometimes labeled internal tautonyms, but we'll simplify and call them double triples. Excluded are reduplicative words that are specifically constructed of repeated elements, such as *cancan, cha-cha, pompom,* and *fifty-fifty.*

Common words that contain double triple patterns include:

al*falfa*	ins*tantan*eous	po*sessed*	stom*achach*e
*assass*in	*kinkin*ess	r*edeede*d	su*perper*fect
*barbar*ic	*murmur*	r*inging*	*testes*
co*ntente*d	para*llell*ed	s*atiat*ion	*tinting*

The hotshot word *hotshots* is the only common one that consists of two touching sets of the same four letters.

IDEALITY

Here eight letters manage to generate five vowels and five syllables. *Oceania,* the collective name for the approximately 25,000 islands of the Pacific, is a capital example of this kind of syllabic density — one letter shorter than *ideality,* yet still containing five vowels and five syllables.

INDIVISIBILITY

The *i*'s have it. The vowel *i* is repeated more frequently in single words than any other letter, such as in the four- *i*'ed *civilizing, infinitive,* and *initiation;* the five *i*'ed *initializing, invincibility,* and *invisibility;* and the six *i*'d *indivisibility.* There are those who would catch your eyes with seven *i*'s in *indivisibilities,* a word that strikes us as a bit contrived.

The letter *s* clearly wins the prize for frequency of a consonant, showing up five times in the likes of *assesses* (the longest string in a word that uses only one consonant), six times in *possessiveness,* and eight times in *possessionlessness.*

With pride, the Word Circus presents a parade of the other twenty-four letters, with examples of words in which each letter pops up and out most frequently. Note how *j, q, v,* and *x* don't like hanging out with their own kind:

A: abracadabra (5)

B: babble (3)

C: concupiscence (4)

D: fuddy-duddy (5)

E: beekeeper (5)

F: riffraff (4)

G: giggling (4)

H: hashish (3)

J: jejune (2)

K: knickknack (4)

L: hillbilly (4)

M: mammogram (4)

N: nonintervention (5)

O: photocomposition (5)

P: pepper-upper (5)

Q: quinquennial (2)

R: referrer (4)

T: statuette (4)

U: muumuu (4)

V: savvy (2)

W: powwow (3)

X: executrix (2)

Y: syzygy (3)

Z: pizzazz (4)

Another five-*n* word is *inconveniencing,* in which all the *n*'s appear three letters away from each other.

KINNIKINNIK

This mixture of sumac leaves, dogwood bark, and bearberry smoked by Cree Native Americans in the Ohio Valley presents us with the longest English natural palindromic word.

Among longer "English" palindromes is the eleven-letter *detartrated,* "separated from or free of tartaric acid." Similar is the ten-letter *detannated* — "separated from or free of tannin." As coined scientific terms, *detartrated* and *detannated* are more sideshow oddities than Big Top attractions.

Beyond English there is *Malayalam,* a Dravidian language related to Tamil and spoken on the Malabar coast of India, presumably in palindromes.

Although it appears in no dictionary, the fifteen-letter Finnish word *saippuakauppias* and the nineteen-letter *saippuakivikauppias,* designating a soap or lye dealer, are, according to native speakers of the language, grammatically sanctioned compound words. They beat the closest English language example by four letters and are recognized by the *Guinness Book of World Records* as the longest palindromic words.

LACERATED

Lacerated can be charaded not only as LACE RATED, but as a trio of successive three-letter words that build a three-by-three word square, with the components reading horizontally and three other words materializing vertically:

L A C
E R A
T E D

LLAMA

The only common English word that begins with a double consonant:

A one-L lama lives to pray.
A two-L llama pulls a dray.
A three-L ama's kind of dire.
A four-L ama's one big fire!

If you went to the mall to purchase a certain South American ruminant, you would then own *a mall llama,* creating a palindromic string of four consecutive consonants.

lillypilly

The letters *bdfghijkpqtyz* are called extenders because in lowercase type or cursive they poke their heads or feet above or below the line. Lowercase and cursive *j* and cursive *f* are the only ones that protrude in both directions.

Among words composed entirely of extenders the most extensive is the ten-letter *lillypilly,* a tall Australian tree with fine, hard-grained wood. Given the obscurity of *lillypilly,* you may prefer *flightily* (nine letters), *filthify* and *filthily* (eight letters), or the more familiar *flighty, lightly,* and *tightly* (all seven letters).

Words fraught with descenders — *fgjpqyz* — might be called lowdown words. They're rare because none of the major vowels drags a tail below the line. The best lowdown word is *syzygy,* which is not only bereft of a major vowel but is formed from five consecutive descenders.

LOLL

Several four-letter words share first prize for containing the greatest density of a particular letter. *I, a,* and *o* represent 100% of a single letter, as do any of the other letters in the alphabet. Beyond that penetrating glimpse into the obvious, 75% of *épée, loll, lull,* and *sass* consists of a single letter.

MAINLAND

What are the longest words that we can cobble by stringing together a series of two-letter state postal abbreviations? "Stately words" of four letters abound, from *AKIN* (Arkansas + Indiana) to *GAME* (Georgia + Maine) to *ORAL* (Oregon + Alabama) to *WINE* (Wisconsin + Nebraska). About twenty combinations of six letters can be found, from *ALMOND* (Alabama + Missouri + North Dakota) to *INCOME* (Indiana + Colorado + Maine) to *VANDAL* (Virginia + North Dakota + Alabama).

Eight-letter strings are rare as black pearls. In fact, the only common examples of such postal-abbreviation words are *CONCORDE* (Colorado + North Carolina + Oregon + Delaware), *GANYMEDE* (Georgia + New York + Maine + Delaware), *MANDARIN* (Massachusetts + North Dakota + Arkansas + Indiana), *MEMORIAL* (Maine + Missouri + Rhode Island + Alabama), and — ta da! — *MAINLAND* (Massachusetts + Indiana + Louisiana + North Dakota).

Some stately words are composed of overlapping abbreviations, in which the second letter of each shortening overlaps with the first letter of the next one: *MARINE* = Massachusetts + Arkansas + Rhode Island + Indiana + Nebraska.

NONSUPPORTS

Here we have the longest word (eleven letters) cobbled entirely of letters from the second half of the alphabet. *Untrustworthy* (thirteen letters) is a frustrating near miss because we can't get the *h* out of there.

RESTAURATEURS

By far the longest (thirteen letters) balanced word, that is, a word in which a single middle letter, acting as a fulcrum, is surrounded by an identical set of letters. In *restaurateurs,* the middle *r* is both preceded and followed by the letters *aerstu.*

If one sets the requirement that the surrounding letters must appear in the same order on both sides of the midpoint, the champion words are *eighty-eight* and *artsy-fartsy,* both eleven letters. Runners up, but perhaps more impressive because they are not obvious repetitions, are the nine-letter *outshouts* and *outscouts.* The seven-letter *ingoing* is nicely camouflaged.

Abracadabra (eleven letters) is a distant and distinguished relative of this category — two occurrences of the four-letter *abra,* with a *cad* in between.

RHYTHMS

The longest word lacking an *a, e, i, o,* or *u, rhythms* boasts two syllables, yet only one vowel. Also syllabically efficient are *schism* (and any other kind of ism, from *fascism* to *romanticism*), *dirndl, fjord, subtly, massacring,* and *Edinburgh,* each characterized by fewer vowels than syllables.

SENSUOUSNESS

Some palindromic letter patterns repose inside a word, anchored there by other letters. Five-letter anchored palindromes are relatively common, including this dozen:

b*anana*	*dissid*ent	h*angna*il	p*ropor*tion
bre*athta*king	di*visiv*e	h*elple*ss	*rever*e
c*hocoh*olic	ev*ergre*en	p*etite*	s*ynony*m

Now step right up to a dozen six-letter anchored palindromes:

b*raggar*t	*grammar*	mo*delled*	s*taccat*o
*diffid*ent	k*nittin*g	pos*sesses*	*tinnit*us
fiddl*edeede*e	mi*sdeeds*	sh*redder*	u*nessen*tial

Ta da! Here now are one last dozen anchored palindromes, each of seven letters:

*assessa*ble	i*gniting*	m*onotono*us	reco*gnizing*
f*ootstoo*l	in*terpret*	p*acifica*tion	r*edivide*
hu*llabal*loo	l*ocofoco*	pr*ecipice*	*selfles*s

But the grand champion of all anchored palindromes — ahead of its closest competitor by four letters — is the eleven-letter sequence embedded in *sensuousnes*s.

SEQUOIA

The shortest word (seven letters) in which each major vowel appears once and only once. Eight-letter exhibits include *dialogue* and *equation*. *Sequoia* is further distinguished by a string of four consecutive vowels.

One up on *sequoia* is the word *queueing,* marked by five consecutive vowels. *Miaou* is listed in some dictionaries as an alternate spelling of *meow*. The past tense of *miaou* is *miaoued* — a seven-letter word that features an unbroken string of the five major vowels!

SHANGHAIINGS

The longest reasonably familiar word (twelve letters) that consists entirely of letter pairs — two *s*'s, two *h*'s, two *a*'s, two *n*'s, two *g*'s, and two *i*'s.

Among eight-letter exhibits are *appeases, hotshots, reappear, signings,* and *teammate.* Among ten-letter runners-up we find *arraigning, horseshoer,* and *intestines.* In many of these isogrammatic words, the two halves contain the same letters and hence are anagrams of each other.

SLEEVELESS

The best example of a pyramid word, containing one occurrence of one letter, two occurrences of a second letter, and so on. Six-letter, 1-2-3 examples abound:

acacia	bowwow	hubbub	pepper
banana	cocoon	mammal	tattoo
bedded	horror	needed	wedded

Ten-letter, four-layer pyramids are wondrous monuments. Packed in *sleeveless* are one *v,* two *l*'s, three *s*'s, and four *e*'s. The strata in *Tennessee's* are one *t,* two *n*'s, three *s*'s, and four *e*'s.

STRENGTHLESSNESS

The longest common univocalic word — one that contains just one vowel repeated (sixteen letters, three *e*'s). Next is *defenselessness* (fifteen letters, five *e*'s).

STRENGTHS

One of a number of nine-letter words of one syllable and the longest containing but a single vowel. Among its strengths is the fact that it ends with five consecutive consonants.

Nine-letter, one-syllable words with more than one vowel include:

scratched   screeched   scrounged   squelched   stretched

Squirreled is the longest one-syllable word (eleven letters), if you indeed pronounce it monosyllabically.

The lengthiest two-syllable words come to thirteen letters:

breakthroughs   breaststrokes   straightedged   straightforth

The twelve-letter *spendthrifts* merits a merit badge because it may the longest word that is pronounced exactly as it is spelled.

SUPEREROGATORILY

The longest word (sixteen letters) that alternates consonants and vowels. Runners-up are the fourteen-letter *verisimilitude* and the thirteen-letter *ineligibility*. *Sweetheart* is a sweetheart of a word that alternates consonant pairs and vowel pairs. *Cloakrooms* and *steamboats* are the only other common ten-letter examples.

When we seek to find the longest word that can be typed on a single horizontal row of a standard typewriter keyboard, we naturally place our fingers on the top row of letters — *qwertyuiop* — because five of the seven vowels reside there. From that single row we can type but a handful of ten-letter words: *repertoire, proprietor, perpetuity, pepperroot, pepperwort,* and — ta da! — *typewriter.*

The longest middle-row words are *flagfalls* (nine letters) and *alfalfas* (eight letters). *Stewardesses, aftereffects, desegregated,* and *reverberated,* all twelve letters, are the longest words than can be

typed with just the left hand, while *johnny-jump-up* (twelve letters, a variety of pansy) is the longest right hand word. The thirteen-letter *dismantlement* and the ten-letter *skepticism* sinisterly and dextrously alternate hands.

UNCOPYRIGHTABLE

An isogram is a single word in which no letter of the alphabet appears more than once — an iso(lated pan)gram. Among fairly common English words, the fifteen-letter *uncopyrightable* is the longest. In *uncopyrightable* each major vowel plus *y* appears once and only once.

The less familiar *dermatoglyphics* (the science of skin patterns, especially fingerprints) also sports fifteen letters. *Ambidextrously* is a satisfying fourteen-letter isogram; it too contains each major vowel plus *y*. The eleven-letter *palindromes* receives extremely honorable mention.

The longest isographic duo is *blacksmith-gunpowdery* (twenty letters), the longest trio (twenty-two letters) *frowzy-humpbacks-tingled,* which is also a plausible sentence.

UNDERGROUND

It's shockingly easy to turn your *mentor* into your *tormentor:* Simply clone the *tor* at the end and graft the offspring on to the beginning of the word. Even more subtly, buried in *underground* are the letters *und* at both the beginning and the end. And, if you accept *undergrounder* as a word, you have an entity beginning and ending with *under.*

Many other words begin and end with the same trigram, including:

antioxidant	*entertainment*	*mesdames*	*rediscovered*
bedaubed	*ionization*	*microcosmic*	*restores*

WELL-EXPRESSED

How many times a year do you answer or dial (or push or punch or poke) the telephone? Chances are that your annual telephonic visits number in the thousands. Yet can you identify, without going to a telephone, which two letters of the alphabet are missing from your telephone dial?

Here's some more telephonic logology: The longest word that can be dialed (pushed? punched? poked?) using only letters that appear with odd numerals on a standard telephone is *well-expressed* (9-355-3977-37733). The longest word that can be dialed using only letters that appear with even numerals is *noncommunicating* (666-266-6864-228464). As with the word

WHICH TWO LETTERS ARE MISSING FROM YOUR TELEPHONE DIAL?

typewriter, we behold [*Twilight Zone* theme music] an eerie confluence of letter configuration and meaning.

Name some pairs of seven-letter words that can be dialed (pushed? punched? poked?) on a telephone with the same number without having any letters in the same position. Try 278-7433 and you'll reach *astride* and *brushed/crushed.* Try 266-8687 for *amounts* and *contour,* another pair with no overlapping letters. *Pygmies* and *swinger* (794-6437) come close, save for the penultimate *e* in each.

Oh yes. The missing telephonic letters are *q* and *z.*

MARY HAD

A LETTER LAMB

Ladies and gentlemen! Children from eight to eighty! Beyond the Big Top you'll find the concession stands, where you can:

> Feast your eyes and gorge your ears and lick
>   Your lips at apple words perched on a stick —
> Popped-buttery words, words like roasted peanuts,
>   Words to satiate all A-B-C nuts.

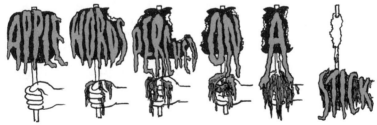

> Syrupy, fizzy words. Don't walk, please run,
>   For steaming hot-dog words, snug in a bun;
> Chocolate-covered words; and pink words spun
>   Sweet as cotton candy. Oh, what fun!

After the food booths, you come to the petting zoo, with its cuddly calves, goats, and deer. There crowds flock and flocks crowd to see one of the star attractions of the circus — Mary's letter lamb.

Perhaps the most famous of all poems for little boys and girls is the eight lines of verse composed by Sarah Josepha Hale and published in 1830 in *Poems for Our Children:*

to school one day,

That was against the rule;

RULE NO. 1:
NO LAMBS

It made the children laugh

HA HA HO HE
HE HE HE HA HA HE
HA HE HO HA HA HE
HO HA HO HA HA HO

and play

To see a lamb at school.

We wonder if Sarah Josepha would hail the things that happen to her letter lamb when verbivores attack it. In each of the fifteen versions that you are about to view, the logopoet uses a specific form of letter recreation to rewrite Sarah Josepha Hale's creation. The trick is to stay within the rules of each letter pattern while preserving the spirit and general form of the original poem. We hope that the wild-and-woolly ram-ifications will appeal to all you dyed-in-the-wool logolepts.

Let's start with an acrostic in which the first letters of the first stanza spell MARY and the first letters of the second row LAMB:

Mary had a little lamb,
   A ram with fleece like snow;
Reacting to where Mary went,
   Young lamb was sure to go;

Lamb followed her to school one day,
   A flouting of the rule;
Making children laugh and play,
   Beholding lamb at school.

"Baah," you bleat sheepishly. "That variation wasn't very difficult." We agree that the joke's on ewe. But in *Word Ways,* February 1989, A. Ross Eckler, the magazine's editor, far exceeded the simple acrostic by composing a double quatrain in which the initial letters of each word replicate the first six-plus words of the poem itself:

Mary acquired ram yesterday —
   A coat quite unblemished.
It romps each day,
   Runs alongside Mary.

Yes, each school teacher expels rams
   Daintily accompanying youths,
Although children often amused,
   Teacher quite unimpressed.

Now read our lipograms. A lipogram is a statement or poem from which a key letter has been excluded. For example, the following poem contains every letter in the alphabet save one. What is the missing letter?

A jovial swain
Should not complain
Of any buxom fair
Who mocks his pain
And thinks it gain
To quiz his awkward air.

The absent letter is *e.*

In *Word Ways,* August 1969, logomagician Eckler presented "Mary Had a Lipogram," in which he demonstrated that it is possible to rewrite literature lipogrammatically. In each merry "Mary," Dr. Eckler banished a common letter — successively *e, a, t, s, h,* and then a large cluster — and still preserved both sense and meter. Here is Eckler's lipogrammatic version with *e,* the most frequently used letter in the alphabet, omitted:

Mary had a tiny lamb,
   Its wool was pallid as snow;
And any spot that Mary did walk
   This lamb would always go.

This lamb did follow Mary to school,
   Although against a law;
How girls and boys did laugh and play
   That lamb in class all saw.

And without *a:*

Polly owned one little sheep,
   Its fleece shown white, like snow;
Every region where Polly went
   The sheep did surely go;

He followed her to school one day
   (Which broke the rigid rule);
The children frolicked in their room
   To see the sheep in school.

To show the possibilities of alphabetic compression, Eckler exiled at a stroke *b, f, g, j, k, o, q, u, v, w, x, y,* and *z* — half the letters of the alphabet!:

> Maria had a little sheep,
>   As pale as rime its hair;
> And all the places Maria came
>   The sheep did tail her there;
>
> In Maria's class it came at last
>   (A sheep can't enter there).
> It made the children clap their hands;
>   A sheep in class, that's rare!

Just as the foregoing lipograms bar specific letters, the univocalic excludes all vowels but one. For example, the following couplet about the Ten Commandments employs only the vowel *e:*

> Preserve these perfect tenets, men;
> Ever keep these precepts ten.

For "Mary Had a Little Lamb," Paul Hellweg, in *Word Ways,* August 1986, performed the same feat with *e*'s:

> Meg kept the wee sheep,
>   The sheep's fleece resembled sleet;
> Then wherever Meg went
>   The sheep went there next;
>
> He went where she heeded her texts,
>   The precedent he neglected;
> The pre-teens felt deep cheer
>   When the sheep entered there.

In *Anguish Languish* (Prentice-Hall, 1956), Howard L. Chace invented a method of double-sound punnery to narrate furry tells (fairy tales) and noisier rams (nursery rhymes). Using this loopy language, Chace replaced the words in the original versions with words that are similar but never quite the same in sound. Here the first stanza is Chace's, the second ours. Oriole ratty? Den less gat stuttered!:

Marry hatter ladle limb.
  Itch fleas worse widest snore;
An ever-wear debt Marry win
  Door limb worse shorter gore.

High fallow dear tusk cool wand hay.
  Thought wars aghast door who'll;
Id meade thatch hill drain lift and plea
  Deuce he a limb ads cool.

Ross Eckler followed his lanolin-fraught tour de farces with "Mary Had a Pangrammatic Lamb," in *Word Ways*, February 1989. Note that every letter of the alphabet appears at least once:

Mary had a little lamb
  With fleece extremely white;
Instead of grazing, all alone,
  The lamb kept out of sight.

He followed her to school one day,
  Which was against the rule.
The children thought it quite a joke
  To view a lamb at school.

In the same issue of *Word Ways,* appeared a version by James Rambo in which the two stanzas are anagrams of each other:

> A girl once kept a tiny sheep,
>   Widely famed for whiteness;
> This pet would dog her every step,
>   No certain sign of brightness.
>
> 'Twas viewed, the pest, one day in class
>   By impish children there;
> Kids laugh to see pets, goofing off,
>   Weren't trying — open, err!

Dr. Eckler also gave the world a heteroliteral version, in which each word has no letters in common with the words that immediately precede and follow it:

> Mary owned a tiny ewe;
>   Its fleece was much like snow.
> But everywhere big Mary went,
>   Small ewe did surely go.

It came to class one day in May,
 Despite a rule "No ewe";
Alas, the class did jump with glee
 To have young lamb on view.

Eckler yoked his heteroliteral lamb to its homoliteral sibling. Now each word has at least one letter in common with the following word:

Mary had a baby lamb,
 As pale as frost her fur;
Whenever Mary ventured forth,
 That lamb accompanied her.

He went along to school one time
 (This was against the rule);
The children laughed and clapped their hands —
 Lambs should stay out of school.

This performance has inspired the Word Circus to accept an even more daunting homoliterary challenge. Within each line, the last letter of each word is also the first letter of the word that follows:

Maria acquired diminutive ewe
Of fleece emitting glow.
Whatever realm Maria accessed,
The ewe'd, delighting, go.

So ovine entered damsel's school,
Trespassing 'gainst their rule;
Children nickered, dawdled, danced —
So ovine exits school.

Peter Newby made up the first line of a palindromic version, and Dave Morice completed the first verse in *Word Ways*, November 1990. Now is the time to finish the challenge with an original second verse. Typically, a palindromic parody takes us into some bizarre pastures:

Mary bred a Derby ram,
Won some gem o' snow.
Went one romp more, not new
O gods, Mary, rams do go!

Walks a ton, not ask law —
'Loof drag gal, laggard fool.
Mar damn mad ram
Loots Mary, ram, stool.

Even more palindramatically, Dave Morice, in *Word Ways,* November 1988, has turned the entire poem, from start to finish, into a two-way narrative:

Mary, baboon? to go to room?
Gnu? Star? No, 'tis all lamb.
O, bit on stool, eh, Mary?
Won, sore heel? Sit! One rule, so:

No nose lure. No, 'tis Lee, hero,
  Snowy ram. He loots! Not I, Bob.
Mall, la, sit on rat. Sung —
  "Moo rot! O, got no, O baby, ram!"

As a not-so-secret coda to the sensational, recreational fun with Mary and her letter lamb, we'll spoonerize you with a gag:

Larry lad a middle ham.
  Flits niece was sight as woe.
And every there what wary meant,
  The gam was lure to show.

He hollowed fur to school done way,
  Watch whiz arraignst the ghoul.
Skit plaid the ildren chaff and may
  Sue lee a scam at tool.

Ladies and gentlemen! I'm grateful that you have allowed me to to pull your eyes over the wool. I thank you for being willing to gamble by gamboling through our letter-pattern verse. To err is human, but to mess around with letters is simply ovine! And with those puns, we'll take it on the lamb.

A
LETTER-PERFECT
SIDESHOW

Outside the Big Top stand the sideshows. There men and women and boys and girls of all ages strain to see the capacious and hippo-condria-cal Fat Lady; the Human Skeleton, who makes no bones about giving you the skinny; the preposterone-pumped Strong Man; the illustrated multi-media Tattooed Man; the herpetological Snake Charmer, who works for scales; the Bearded Lady, who always wins by a whisker by earning her bread with her bared beard; the India Rubber Man, who bends over backwards beyond any stretch of the imagination; and the gender-ender hermaphrodite, who combines the best of both worlds.

Jest for the pun of it, audiences look up to the Giant, whose positive alti-tude reaches new heights of entertainment; the Dog-Faced boy who performs in the pup tent and is studying to become a barker; the Elephant Man from Tusk-a-looser, who sways to the trunk-ated music of Harry Elephante and Elephant Gerald; the Egyptian Princess of a thousand veils — always in a state of De Nile; the hip Siamese Twins, who take periodic trips to England so that the other one can drive; the sword swallower, on the cutting edge as he eats a sword and his words; the Alligator Man; the Lobster Boy; the Mule-Faced Girl; the Wild Man of Borneo; and other exotic attractions bound to evoke your admission that they are more than worth the price of admission.

Ladies and gentlemen! Boys and girls! Step out of the main tent and tour an exhibition of the world's most spectacular words, those fantastic freaks of nature and confounding curiosities:

A

This being a letter-perfect attraction, we'll start by having a look at the logology of our letters. More than half the letters in the alphabet sound like words:

A: a
B: be, bee
C: sea, see
G: gee
I: aye, eye, I
J: jay

K: quay
L: el
M: em
N: en
O: O, oh, owe
P: pea, pee

Q: cue, queue
R: are
T: tea, tee
U: ewe, yew, you
X: ex
Y: why

and all letters can be used as kickoffs to everyday words:

A-frame
B-movie
C-section
D-day
E-mail
F-stop
G-string
H-bomb
I beam
J-bar
K ration

L-dopa
M phase

N-type
O-ring

Q ←O-RING
←Q-TIP

P-wave
Q-Tip
R-month
S-curve
T-shirt
U-turn
V-neck
W-particle
X-ray
Y-chromosome
Z-coordinate

Let's examine a few characters for their special characteristics:

*C is one of six letters that when pronounced as plurals sound like
words that aren't themselves plural:

C's: seize   E's: ease   G's: Geez   P's: pease   T's: tease   Y's: wise

*E is the most common letter occurring in English. In fact, one out of
eight printed letters is an *e*. The sound of E is embedded in the pronunciation of eight other letters — *B, C, D, G, P, T, V,* and *Z.*

*H is the only letter that has no word or words that rhyme with it. *A,*
for example, has *bay, day,* and dozens of other rhyme words, and *W,* for
another example, has "trouble you." But *H* is rhymeless. Also, *H* is first
in line alphabetically when the letters are spelled out phonetically —
aitch, are, ay, bee, cue, dee, double yoo, and so on.

*I am here to tell you that English is the only major language to capital-
ize its first-person singular pronoun. Some observers believe that such
capitalization brings about a linguistic egocentrism, a sort of "beauty is
in the *I* of the beholder" complex. As evidence, note that *I* is the most
frequently spoken word in English.

*U is the only major vowel that, when sounded, begins
with a consonant: — *yoo.*

*W is the shortest three-syllable word
in English, and none of the letters in "double-u" is a *w.* All
other letters of the alphabet are
sounded with just a single syllable.

BEAUTY IS IN THE **I** OF THE BEHOLDER

THE FABULOUS FIFTY-TWO-FINGERED
FORTUNE ★ TELLER

ACE KING QUEEN JACK TEN NINE EIGHT SEVEN SIX FIVE FOUR THREE TWO

DIGITAL DELIA

THE ONLY PERSON IN
THE WORLD WHO CAN
COUNT ON ONE HAND
ALL 52 LETTERS
IN A DECK OF CARDS!

*According to the Word Circus X Files, the letter *X* can be pronounced in at least nine different ways, depending on context:

eks: x-ray   *ks:* hex
gz: exist   *ksh:* anxious
gzh: luxurious   *z:* xylophone
k: except   __: faux pas
kris: Xmas

ACE

In *ace,* the first, third, and fifth letters of the alphabet are joined. Ho hum, you yawn, and I agree because I haven't been playing with a full deck. I'm a jack ace who ought to be dealt with, you say to yourself. But think upon this: If you add up the number of letters in that deck — *ace king queen jack ten nine eight seven six five four three two* — the total comes to fifty-two!

ALBUQUERQUE

A distinctive city name in that the letter *q,* which has almost no multiple uses, occurs twice and *u* three times. Moreover, the *que* is pronounced in two different ways.

ALKALINE

Can anyone ever top the combination of charade and famous name in alkaline/AL KALINE, the Hall of Fame outfielder for the Detroit Tigers? Our sideshow extravaganza offers an exhibit of logological manipulations beyond those presented in "Big-Name Acts":

* *Theda Bara,* the film name of one Theodosia Goodman, combines an anagram and a semordnilap for *Arab Death.*

* The surname of French existentialist writer Albert *Camus* becomes the semordnilap *Sumac,* which happens to be not only a rash plant, but the last name of Camus' contemporary, singer Yma Sumac. Had the two actually met, onlookers might have observed, CAMUS SEES SUMAC.

Agamemnon, the name of the mythical Greek king so prominent in the *Iliad* and other literary masterpieces, is constructed from three three-letter palindromes:

AGA   MEM   NON

*Many first and last names are multiple loopers. Thus, the surname of tennis legend Arthur *Ashe,* after whom a tennis stadium is named, can be looped into *Shea,* the name of another and nearby sports venue. Other loopers:

Alban/banal	Chet/etch	Levi/evil	Teddie/dieted
Alsop/opals	Dale/Leda	Lyon/only	Vera/rave
Ande/Dean	Derry/Ryder	Norma/manor	Verdi/divers
Berger/Gerber	Diana/Nadia	Otto/toot	Verne/never
Cain/Inca	Eddy/dyed	Reba/bare	Vespa/paves

*The surname of New York Yankees star pitcher Andy P*ettitte* contains a seven-letter embedded palindrome.

*Scooting the *s* across the space separating the first and last name of a celebrity reveals something about the celebrity. In each case, the result is a special kind of charade rearrangement:

Garry's handling	Loretta's wit	Soupy's ales
Gloria's wan son	Robert's tack	Sylvester's tall one
Larry's torch	Sharon's tone	Tom and Dick's mothers

Al Gore's name becomes *galore* when spoonerized, then GAL ORE when charaded. Mr. Gore becomes an *ogre* when his name is turned inside out. That's what we call an Al Gore rhythm.

*When spoonerized, *Rip Van Winkle* turns into the elderly lion tamer *Whip Van Wrinkle.*

*In the film *Batman and Robin,* the villainous villainess Poison Ivy is played by *Uma Thurman,* whose first name is concealed as a joey in her last name.

*Is it simply a pathetic fallacy that *phallus* in pig Latin is *Alice Faye?*

*Movie stars *Judith Anderson, Bela Lugosi, Rosalind Russell, Blair Underwood,* tennis stars *Gussie Moran* and *Guillermo Vilas,* golfer *Justin Leonard,* and Civil War general *Ambrose Burnside* (who eponymously bequeathed us the word for those sweeping sidewhiskers) are among the luminaries whose first and last names together contain all the major vowels. Is there a more compactly voweled surname than that of Grace *Metalious,* author of *Peyton Place?*

*One reason that San Diego Padres outfielder *Tony Gwynn* is baseball's best hitter since Ted Williams is that his last name is not weighted down by any major vowels — another benefit of abstemiousness.

*Within the eight letters of *King John,* immortalized by William Shakespeare, reposes the letter string *GHIJK,* along with the nearby *NO.*

*In such classic books as *An Almanac of Words at Play* and *The Word's Gotten Out,* word wizard, letter engineer, poet, and raconteur extraordinaire Willard R. *Espy* guides his readers along the giggle road through the mischief of words. How serendipitous it is that Willard's surname is one of the most logologically incandescent in the onomastic universe. *Espy* is a grammagram — SP — and a letter statement questioning extrasensory perception — ESP? WHY? Perhaps you *espy* and *spy* that *Espy* is also a capitonym and a beheadable synonym.

AVIS

To rent an *Avis* automobile, simply loop the first letter to the end of the word and use your *Visa* card. *Lay's* (potato chips) and *Select* (punch) are also looping anagrams. Such transformations alert us that brand names lend themselves to letter play other than the palindromic and semordnilapic maneuvers that capered through "Big-Name Acts."

Advil (analgesic) anagrams into *valid* and *Aleve* into *leave*, its own homophone minus a syllable.

*If you buy an appliance from *Amana* and pay on the Amana plan, you will have a good start on a famous palindrome: *Amana plan, a canal, Panama!*

*An interpretive kangarooing of *Camry* is MY CAR, of *Renault* REAL NUT, and of *Budweiser* WISER BEER. Will eating *Snickers* make us *sick?*

Dove (chocolate, soap) is a heteronym of the bird.

*An anagram of *Frito-Lay* is I FRY A LOT.

Nivea (moisturizer) is an anagram of *Evian* (mineral water) and NAFTA may help *Fanta* (soft drink) to gain consumers internationally.

Palmolive (soap) can be cleft charadefully into PALM OLIVE and *Caterpillar* (tractor) into CATER PILLAR. When curtailed and then charaded, *Frigidaire* (refrigerator) becomes FRIGID AIR. *Petsmart* (pet supplies) divides both into PETS' MART or PET SMART.

*Manufactured from one *r*, two *s*'s, and three *e*'s, *Reese's* (candy) is a pyramid word.

Rolex (watches) is a joey of *Rolodex* (file card holder).

Scope (mouthwash) can be looped to form the statement SCOPE COPES.

*Behead *Spam* (ham) and you end up with *Pam* (cooking oil).

* *Tostitos* begins and ends with the same trigram.

* *Touchtone* (telephones) is both a joey and homophone of *touchstone*.

* *Tylenol* (analgesic), *Pepsi* (cola), and *Yamaha* (motorcycles) are among the product names that cry out to be palindromed into enthusiastic slogans:

> LONELY TYLENOL
>
> PEPSI IS PEP.
>
> AHA, MAY, A YAMAHA.

AYE

Aye can be anagrammatically looped into its own synonym *yea*. These two English words share no letters with their French cousin *oui*, yet together they encompass the six common vowels.

Another affirmative-action word is *Ouija*, the trademark for a popular board game. This name was coined in 1891 from the French *oui*, "yes," and the German *ja*, "yes." The game is usually pronounced *weejee*, with two long *ee* sounds, yet the spelling of *Ouija* includes every major vowel but *e*.

BEDLAM

More than just one letter at a time can leap from front word to back word to form a looping anagram. Excluded are reverse compounds, such as *boathouse/houseboat, huntsman/manhunts, Passover/overpass,* and *shotgun/gunshot;* particle verbs, such as *takeout/outtake* and *upset/setup;* and repetitions, such as *yo-yo, fifty-fifty,* and *pretty-pretty.*

We can command a cluster of two letters to leapfrog over two other letters so that the two pairs switch places:

arch/char	arts/tsar	chit/itch	eddy/dyed	game/mega
arse/sear	chin/inch	code/deco	emit/item	mesa/same

Now watch three letters leap and loop across two letters:

bowel/elbow	cedar/arced	ideas/aside	mitre/remit	sonar/arson
braze/zebra	glean/angle	loyal/alloy	route/utero	verse/sever

Perhaps the most intriguing of these three-two transposals is the contrasting *jihad* (a holy war)/ *hadji* (a holy man).

Next, four letters will vault over two others:

ablest/stable	centre/recent	pineal/alpine	ranter/errant

The most balanced of multiple loops is three letters bounding over three other letters, producing a three-three switch:

bedlam/lambed	German/manger	Nassau/saunas
callow/low-cal	Lothar/harlot	rowing/ingrow

Finally, two four-three transposals – *raining/ingrain* and *pinking/kingpin.*

BROUGHAM

The *ugha* in *brougham* constitutes the longest sequence of silent letters in a word. The *gh* in *taught* is the longest string of letters that can be deleted to produce a homophone, here *taut.* (Excluded are weird names, such as the British *Featherstone-Haux,* pronounced *Fanshaw!*)

A ship's *forecastle* is sometimes written as *fo'c's'le,* making it the most apostrophisized of our words (just ask the bo's'n) and one with three clusters of silent letters.

CHRISTCHURCH

Christchurch, the most English city in New Zealand, contains ten consonants (clustered 3-4-3) and only two vowels, an astonishing 5-1 ratio.

CITRUS

A delicious six-letter example of an inside-out word. Unfold *citrus* from the middle to the outer skin, making the order of the letters 4-5-6, 3-2-1, and the adjective *rustic* appears. Open up *lemons* from the middle — 3-2-1, 4-5-6 — and you taste *melons*. Also worthy of mention is the 4-5-6, 3-2-1 pair *circle/cleric*.

CONVERSATIONALISTS
Paired with *conservationalists,* this is the longest non-scientific anagram.

CORPSE
Subtract an e from *corpse,* a word that ends with a silent letter, and you'll come up with *corps,* a word characterized by two silent letters. Other examples of fascinating body language include:

Arm is one of more-than-you-might-guess body parts spelled with just three letters. Lend your ear to and cast your eye on *ear, eye, gum, hip, jaw, leg, lip, rib, toe,* and (more marginally) *fat, gut, lap, lid,* and a plural — *ova.*

Ear is one of an amazing number of body parts that anagram into another word, *are* and *era* in this case. Other examples:

arch/char
arm/mar/ram
beard/bared/bread
bosom/booms
breast/barest
bust/stub
chin/inch
dimple/limped
face/cafe
flesh/shelf
finger/fringe
gum/mug
gut/tug
heart/earth/hater

PALM LAMP

knee/keen
lap/pal
leg/gel
liver/viler
lobe/bole
nail/lain
nape/pane
navel/venal
node/done
nose/eons
organ/groan
palm/lamp
pate/tape
pore/rope

scalp/claps/clasp
sinew/swine/wines
skin/inks/sink
sole/lose/sloe
spine/pines/snipe
testes/tsetse
toenail/elation
torso/roots
uterus/suture
vein/vine
waist/waits
wrist/writs

Eye is the only palindromic body part.

Intestines is the most logologically exciting of all body components. Its first five letters are an anagram of its second five; both halves are anagrams of the word *inset;* and, in the manner of joey and kangaroo, *testes* hides inside *intestines.*

Palate is one of those body parts that generate homophonically, in this case *pallet* and *palette.* Other corporeal homophones include:

cell/sell	knee/nee	skull/scull
eye/aye/I	muscle/mussel	sole/soul
hair/hare	navel/naval	toe/tow
heart/hart	nose/knows/no's	vein/vain/vane
heel/heal	pore/poor/pour	waist/waste

DEALT

A rare word that anagrams into its own homophone plus one syllable — *delta*. *Muse/emus* is another example, depending on how you pronounce *emus*.

EINSTEIN

The most famous of mnemonic spelling jingles advises:

> *I* before *e*,
> Except after *c*,
> Unless sounded as *a*,
> As in *neighbor* and *weigh*.

You don't have to be an Einstein to realize that the *i*-before-*e* rule is breached as often as it is observed. If you want to find out just how many proper names violate the rule, remember this sentence: "Eugene *O'Neill* and Dwight *Eisenhower* drank a thirty-five-degree-*Fahrenheit Budweiser* and *Reingold* in *Anaheim* and *Leicester*." You also don't have to be an Einstein to see that *Einstein* itself is a double violation (along with *Weinstein, Feinstein, deficiencies, efficiencies, proficiencies,* and *zeitgeist*).

Among the dozens of instances in which *e* precedes *i* in uncapitalized words are this dozen:

caffeine	feisty	kaleidoscope	seize
counterfeit	heifer	leisure	sovereign
either	height	protein	therein

And among words in which *c* is immediately followed by *ie* we note:

ancient	fancier	omniscient	species
concierge	financier	science	sufficient
conscience	glacier	society	tendencies

I Before *E?*

There's a rule that's sufficeint, proficeint, efficeint.
For all speceis of spelling in no way deficeint.
While the glaceirs of ignorance icily frown
This soveriegn rule warms, like a thick iederdown.

On words fiesty and wierd it shines from great hieghts,
Blazes out like a beacon, or skien of ieght lights.
It gives nieghborly guidance, sceintific and fair,
To this nonpariel language to which we are hier.

Now, a few in soceity fiegn to deride
And to forfiet their ancient and omnisceint guide,
Diegn to worship a diety foriegn and hienous,
Whose counterfiet riegn is certain to pain us.

In our work and our liesure, our agenceis, schools,
Let us all wiegh our consceince, sieze proudly our rules!
It's plebiean to lower our standards. I'll niether
Give in or give up – and I trust you won't iether.

FEAST

English is a great multicultural feast of a language, and the various courses of that banquet originated in dozens of other lands — far and near, ancient and modern. So close are the spellings of many of the ancestor words that they can be linked logologically. *Fiesta* (Spanish) anagrams to I FEAST (English) and kangaroos to *festa* (Italian), which curtails to *fest* (German), which substitute-letter transposes to *fete* (French).

FIRST

The only ordinal number whose letters appear in alphabetical order. The only alphabetic cardinal number that matches *first* is *forty.* A number of other "figurative" words have our number:

* *One* is the only number in reverse alphabetical sequence and the only cardinal number formed from a looping anagram — *eon/one.*

* *Four* is the only number with a quantity of letters that matches its value.

* Take from *FIVE* the first, second, and fourth letters and — oh, fie! — you end up with *V,* which still signifies "five."

* Explain the following sequence: 8, 11, 5, 4, 9, 1, 7, 6, 10, 12, 2. These are the first dozen natural numbers listed in alphabetical order, headed by *eight.*

* *Eighth* is the only ordinal number that can be curtailed to yield a cardinal number *(eighth/eight),* the only ordinal number that results from a looping anagram— *height/eighth,* and the only number that contains five consecutive consonants when pluralized *(eighths).*

* *Ten* is the only number that spells a common word when its letters are reversed.

* *Eleven* is the longest number name (six letters) with alternating vowels and consonants; *nine/ten/eleven* make for a thirteen-letter consonant-vowel string.

TEN NET

* *Twelfths* is the longest number word (eight letters) having only one vowel.

* *Seventeen* is the last of all numbers (*three, seven, ten,* and *eleven* are the others) whose names are spelled with *e* as the only vowel.

* In capitalized form, the letters in TWENTY-NINE consist entirely of straight lines – twenty-nine of them to be exact.

* *Eighty-one* is one of only two square-root words, in which the number of letters (nine) is the square root of the number signified by the word itself. The other square-root word is the ten-letter *one hundred.*

* Quick: You have two minutes to rattle off a series of words that are completely devoid of the letter *a.* Actually, all you have to do is start counting "one-two-three-four-five" and so on. You could progress all the way through *nine hundred and ninety-nine* and never use an *a* — not until you reached *one thousand.*

* *Five thousand* is the longest and highest number that can be spelled isogrammatically — no letter repeated.

FLOCCINAUCINIHILIPILIFICATION

Meaning "the categorizing of something as worthless or trivial," this twenty-nine-letter, twelve-syllable word dates back to 1741 and until 1982 was the longest word in the *Oxford English Dictionary.* While it contains nine *i*'s, it is the longest word devoid of any *e.* It also conceals the seven-letter palindrome *ilipili.*

An honorable runner-up to *floccinaucinihilipilification* in the *OED* is the twenty-seven-letter *honorificabilitudinitatibus,* a Latin ablative plural that literally means "with honor." Shakespeare uses the noun in *Love's Labor's Lost,* where Costard says: "I marvel thy master hath not eaten thee for a word; for thou art not so long by the head as *honorificabilitudinitatibus:* thou are easier swallowed than a flap-dragon." Like *floccinaucinihilipilification, honorificabil-*

The Amazing
Floccipaucinihilipilification
Machine

itudinitatibus is an *i*-full (seven *i*'s) that within its thirteen syllables contains nary a single *e*. In addition, *honorificabilitudinitatibus* has the honorable distinction of being the longest dictionary entry that alternates consonants and vowels throughout.

GHOTI

George Bernard Shaw, who championed the cause of spelling reform, once announced that he had discovered a new way to spell the word *fish*. His fabrication was *ghoti* — *gh* as in enou*gh*, *o* as in w*o*men, and *ti* as in na*ti*on.

There are many other "fish" in the A-B-Sea — *phusi: ph* as in *ph*ysic, *u* as in b*u*sy, *si* as in pen*si*on; *ffess:* o*ff*, pr*e*tty, is*su*e; *ughyce:* la*ugh,* h*y*mn, o*ce*an; *Pfeechsi:* *Pf*eiffer, b*ee*n, fu*chs*ia; *pphiapsh:* sa*pph*ire, marri*a*ge, *ps*haw; *fuiseo:* f*a*t, g*u*ilt, naus*eou*s; *ftaisch:* so*ft*en, vill*ai*n, *sch*wa; *ueiscio:* lie*u*tenant (British pronunciaion), forf*ei*t, con*sci*ous.

We stop here only because the game has become in-*f*-able.

The most pervasive, invasive, and evasive of all word puzzles that make the rounds of folk Xerography and cyberspace is this challenge: "There are three words in the English language that end in *g-r-y.* Two of them are *angry* and *hungry.* What is the third?"

The greatest service the Word Circus staff can perform for our adoring public is to announce here that the *gry* question is a time-wasting linguistic hoax. This poser first slithered onto the American scene in 1975 on the Bob Grant radio talk show on WMCA in New York City. Word mavens have tried to bury *gry* before, but it keeps rising, like some angry, hungry monstrosity from *Tales From the Crypt.*

The answer to the infernal question is that there is no answer — at least no satisfactory answer. The Word Circus advises anybody who happens on the *angry+hungry+?* poser to stop burning time and to move on to a more productive activity, like counting the number of angels on the head of a pin or the reductions in your property taxes.

In unabridged dictionaries are enshrined at least fifty *gry* words in addition to *angry* and *hungry,* and every one of them is either a variant spelling, as in *augry* for *augury,* *begry* for *beggary,* and *bewgry* for *buggery,* or exceedingly obscure, as in *anhungry,* an obsolete synonym for *hungry;* *aggry,* a kind of variegated glass bead much in use in the Gold Coast of West Africa; *puggry,* a Hindu scarf wrapped around the helmet or hat and trailing down the back to keep the hot sun off one's neck; or *gry,* a medieval unit of measurement equaling one-tenth of a line.

Fish in the ABSea

Ghoti

Phusi

Ffess

Ughyce

Pfeechsi

Pphiapsh

Fuiseo

Ftaisch

Ueiscio

There are those who contend that the solution to the *gry* poser is right in front of our faces. All we have to do is focus on the third and fourth sentences in one version of the riddle: "Think of three words ending in *gry*. *Angry* and *hungry* are two of them. There are only three words in the English language. What is the third word? The word is something that everyone uses every day. If you have listened carefully, I have already told you what it is."

The third word in "the English language" is, of course, *language,* which is certainly something we use every day. The whole business about *gry* is just a smoke screen.

Nonsense. Humbug. Balderdash. Baloney. Hogwash. Tripe. Piffle. This interpretation gives linguistic chicanery a bad name. The wording of this statement began appearing twenty years after the hoax wormed its way into public consciousness. The structure is rickety, and there are no quotation marks around "the English language." What we have here is a *post hoc* post hoax.

A more realistically challenging puzzle of this type is "Name a common word, besides *tremendous, stupendous,* and *horrendous,* that ends in *dous.*"

At least thirty-two additional *dous* words repose in various dictionaries: *apodous, antropodous, blizzardous, cogitabundous, decapodous, frondous, gastropodous, heteropodous, hybridous, iodous, isopodous, jeopardous, lagopodous, lignipodous, molybdous, mucidous, multifidous, nefandous, nodous, octapodous, palladous, paludous, pudendous, repandous, rhodous, sauropodous, staganopodous, tetrapodous, thamphipodous, tylopodous, vanadous,* and *voudous.*

But these examples are as arcane as those that purport to solve the *gry* problem.

Still, there is a fourth common word ending in *dous* — *hazardous.*

HEARD
What is the only verb in English that does not end in *e* and that forms its past tense by adding just a *d* to the present-tense verb? Remember folks, you heard it here first.

INFINITE
It means "very, very large." Add five letters to this word — *infinite* + *simal* = *infinitesimal* — and it now means "very, very small."

JASON
An amusing pastime is to string together the first letters of people's names as initials of words in meaningful statements. Lee Iacocca's last name, for example, could be said to represent the first letters of "I Am Chairman Of Chrysler Corporation of America."

The name Jason is composed of the first letters of five successive months — July, August, September, October, November. If James Jason were a DJ on FM/AM radio, the first letters of all twelve months would be represented sequentially:

J. JASON, DJ
FM/AM

JOHN

The name John (or Jon) can be changed phonetically into six different women's names or nicknames simply by changing the vowel sound:

Jan	Jean	Joan
Jane	Jen	June

KINE

The only plural that contains no letter in common with its singular — *cow*. Sure, *kine* is archaic, but in the Word Circus, we're allowed to have archaic and eat it too.

Most English nouns form their plurals by adding *-s* or *-es,* as in *elephants* and *horses.* But two parts of the body, three animals, and three human beings become plurals by changing the vowels in their middle.

You learned earlier in the sideshow that the body parts are *foot/feet* and *tooth/teeth.* Here you discover that the animals are *mouse/mice, louse/lice,* and *goose/geese,* and the humans are *man/men, woman/women,* and *child/children.* In this exclusive category, only *woman* goes from singular to plural by undergoing a change in the sounding of both the vowels that appear in the original word.

Joining this pluralistic society is *rhinoceros,* for which dictionaries list four plurals — *rhinoceroses, rhinoceri, rhinocerotes,* and *rhinoceros.*

The noun *die,* the one that means "a cube used for gambling," is the only common English word that forms its plural by adding a consonant besides *s* in the middle — *dice.* Just as unusual, *jinni,* another spelling of *genie,* becomes a plural by the dropping of its last letter and changing into *jinn.*

LLANFAIRPWLLGWYNGYLLGOGERYCHWYRNDROBWLLLLAN-TYSILIOGOGOGOCH

This is the Welsh name of a village railway station in Anglesey, Gwynedd, Wales, cited in the *Guiness Book of World Records.* Translated, the name means "Saint Mary's Church in a hollow of white hazel, close to a whirlpool and Saint Tysilio's Church and near a red cave."

In addition to being one of the longest of place-names, the fifty-eight-letter cluster contains but one *e.* Hidden in the chain are four consecutive *l*'s, a seven-letter palindrome — *ogogogo* — and a fourteen-letter stretch without a major vowel — *rpwllgwyngyllg.*

Close kin to the Welsh rare bit above is the Native American name for a lake near Webster, Massachusetts — *Chargoggagoggmanchauggogoggchaubunagungamaugg* — which means "You fish on your side; I fish on my side; no-

body fish in the middle." In its middle lurks the seven-letter palindrome — *ggogogg* — composed of the same two letters as the *ogogogo* palindrome embedded in *Llanfair* . . . . Fifteen of its forty-five letters are *g*'s, and not one is an *i* or *e*.

LOGOLOGY

In 1965 Dmitri Borgmann resurrected an old word, *logology*, "the science of words," and gave it a new meaning of recreational letter play. That meaning is embodied in the title of his book *Language on Vacation*. How appropriate that the word denoting the study of words viewed as letter patterns should itself be of such recreational interest. *Logology* encompasses two five-letter anchored palindromes — *logol* and *golog* — and repeats the cluster *log*.

Borgmann points out that *logology* is a beautifully balanced word:

*It alternates between consonant and vowel throughout.

*In its lower case form, its odd letters alternate between poking their heads above the writing line (the two *l*'s) and dragging their tails below that line (the two *g*'s).

*If you assign a value of 1 to the letter *a*, 2 to *b*, and continue up to 26 for *z*, *logology* averages 13.5, the perfect midpoint of the alphabet.

MINE

Mining this possessive pronoun, we discover a trilingual synonymic anagram — *mine* (English), *mein* (German), and *mien* (French).

MISSISSIPPI

In letter patterning, this is clearly the best of the state names, rivaled only by *Tennessee*. Both names contain just one vowel repeated four times univocalically, three sets of double letters, and only four different letters.

But *Mississippi* has the distinction of containing a seven-letter embedded palindrome — *ississi;* three overlapping four-letter palindromes — *issi, issi,* and *ippi;* and a double triple — *ississ.* And each year is crowned a new *Miss Mississippi*, whose title consists of three double triples — *Missmiss, ississ,* and *ssissi* — and only four alphabetic units among its fifteen letters.

Other logological exotica of the states we're in include:

*When the names of the forty-eight contiguous states are alphabetized, half start with A-M and half with N-Z. In addition, exactly one third (sixteen) start with A-L, one third with M-N, and one-third with O-Z. The M-N cluster divides perfectly between M and N.

Arkansas is the longest univocalic state name with the vowel *a* (*Alabama, Alaska,* and *Kansas* are the other three) and the only one-word state name within which appears a second state name, written solidly — *Kansas. West Virginia* is the only two-word state name with this characteristic.

*What begins with a union and ends with a separation? The answer is *Connecticut,* which can be charaded into the oxymoron *Connect I cut.*

Hawaii is the only state with a double vowel. HAWAII is also the longest state whose capital letters are vertically symmetrical and will thus appear the same in a mirror. The other three are IOWA, OHIO, and UTAH.

Iowa is the only state besides *Ohio* that contains three syllables and only one consonant.

Louisiana is the only state with *USA* within its borders.

Maine is the only one-syllable state. The curtailment *Maine/main* is homophonous.

Massachusetts is, with thirteen letters, the longest single-word state name (*North* and *South Carolina* match the length of *Massachusetts* in two words).

Nevada is the only state within whose borders reposes a semordnilapic town — *Adaven. Apollo, PA,* and *Omaha, MO,* are place-name palindromes cobbled from state-name abbreviations.

*Within the borders of *New Hampshire* sit the longest United States place-names consisting of town/city and state — the contiguous *Hillsborough Lower Village, New Hampshire,* and *Hillsborough Upper*

Village, New Hampshire, both thirty-six letters. *Charleston* (South Carolina, West Virginia, etc.) is the longest (ten letters) isogram among well-known cities.

*New Mexico is the longest state name consisting entirely of alternating consonants and vowels (within each word). *Alabama, Arizona, Colorado, Delaware, Oregon, Nevada, Texas,* and *Utah* also adhere to this pattern.

*Ohio is the only state name that begins and ends with the same letter, other than *a (Alabama, Alaska, Arizona)*, the only state name that is crafted entirely from capital letters with horizontal-vertical symmetry, and the only state name that can be typed with just the right hand. *Texas* is the only state name typed with just the left hand.

*It's a foregone conclusion that if you behead and curtail *foregone*, you end up with *Oregon*.

*Pennsylvania is the only state name keyed with all eight of the typewriter fingers.

*The only letter that does not appear in the name of any state is *q*.

*South Dakota is the only state that shares no letters with its own capital — *Pierre*.

PNEUMONOULTRAMICROSCOPICSILICOVOLCANOCONIOSIS

This hippopotomonstrosesquipedalian word is the longest entered in *Webster's Third New International Dictionary* and, since 1982, the longest in the *Oxford English Dictionary*. The word describes a miners' disease caused by inhaling too much quartz or silicate dust. Among its forty-five letters and nineteen syllables occur nine *o*'s, surely the record for a letter most repeated within a single word, six *c*'s, but one *e*.

A GIMERICK

IT'S TRUE THAT I HAVE HALITOSIS,

AT LEAST IT'S NOT PNEUMONOULTRAMICROSCOPICSILICOVOLCANIOSIS.

THUS, RATHER THAN FLOCCINAUCINIHILIPILIFICATION,

I FEEL HIPPOPOTOMONSTROSESQUIPEDALIAN ELATION

THAT'S SUPERCALIFRAGILISTICEXPIALIDOCIOUS.

A Gimerick
It's true that I have halitosis,
At least it's not pneumonoultramicroscopicsilicovolcaniosis.
Thus, rather than floccinaucinihilipilification,
I feel hippopotomonstrosesquipedalian elation
That's supercalifragilisticexpialidocious.

The longest words that we are likely to encounter in general text are the twenty-two letter *counterrevolutionaries* and *deinstitutionalization.* Then again there's the bumper sticker with the twenty-seven-letter adverb: "He's not dead. He's just electroencephalographically challenged."

POLK

Beyond the letter engineering in "Big-Name Acts," we find significance swirling inside the names of American chief executives, among which the surname *Polk* is among the most pyrotechnic. *Polk* is one of only four presidential surnames consisting of four letters, the others being *Bush, Ford,* and *Taft.* The four letters of *Polk* parade in reverse alphabetical order and are within six of each other in the alphabet. The full name *James Knox Polk* contains the seven adjacent letters *JKLMNOP.*

Here are some other presidential precedents:

*In contrast to the monosyllabic monikers above, *Eisenhower* is the only presidential surname that contains four syllables and that begins with a vowel other than *A.* The first name of *Ulysses Grant* is the only one among presidents that begins with a vowel other than *A.*

**Ulysses Simpson Grant* and *Rutherford Birchard Hayes* are the only presidential names that contain *a, e, i, o,* and *u* with a *y* to boot.

**Madison, Tyler,* and *Nixon* alternate between consonants and vowels. *James Madison* is the only president whose first *and* last names so alternate.

*The surname of *Millard Fillmore* contains five letters in alphabetical order with one repeated. In addition *Fillmore* can be charaded into two words, *fill/more,* in the manner of *washing/ton, a/dams, jack/son, john/son, ha/yes, gar/field, ho/over,* and *nix/on.*

*The surname of *William Henry* and *Benjamin Harrison* is a semordnilap that might be defined as a negative response to an underling: *No, Sirrah. Taft* begs to be expanded into the palindrome *Taft:fat.*

*Four presidents have had surnames containing *oo* — *Roosevelt, Coolidge, Hoover,* and *Roosevelt.* All these men occupied the Oval Office in the twentieth century, three of them sequentially.

*Four presidents have had alliterative first and last names — *Woodrow Wilson, Calvin Coolidge, Herbert Hoover,* and *Ronald Reagan.* Again, all these men served in the twentieth century.

*Nine presidents with double letters in one of their names served sequentially — *William McKinley, Theodore Roosevelt, William Taft, Woodrow Wilson, Warren Harding, Calvin Coolidge, Herbert Hoover, Franklin Roosevelt,* and *Harry Truman.*

Cleveland, McKinley, Roosevelt, Taft, and *Wilson* were elected sequentially and alphabetically, as were the four-man units of *Adams, Jefferson, Madison,* and *Monroe* and *Coolidge, Hoover, Roosevelt,* and *Truman.*

Taft and *Nixon* are the only presidential surnames that begin and end with the same letter. *Theodore Roosevelt* is the only U.S. president whose full name begins and ends with the same letter.

Rutherford B. Hayes's first name contains the last name of *Gerald Ford. Andrew* and *Lyndon Johnson*'s last name contains the first name of four other presidents — *Adams, Quincy Adams, Tyler,* and *Kennedy.* The middle names of *Ronald Wilson Reagan* and *William Jefferson Clinton* match the last names of two of their predecessors.

*Two pairs of presidents share first and last initials. The first is the father-son team of *John Adams* and *John Quincy Adams.* Reverse the *J. A.* pattern and come up with *Andrew Jackson* and *Andrew Johnson.*

* *Pierce, Grant, Ford, Bush, Carter,* and (in Britain) *Hoover* are all common words when uncapitalized.

*Just as the word *president* is beheadable — *p/resident* — a number of presidential surnames are singly or doubly beheadable — *a/dams, g/r/ant, h/a/yes,* and *t/aft.*

QUEUE

Here we gaze upon a word that can have its last four letters curtailed and still retain its original pronunciation. Performing the same trick with its first four letters beheaded is *aitch.*

SMITHERY

When anagrammed, *smithery* contains no fewer than seventeen pronouns:

he	his	its	she	them
her	I	me	their	they
hers	it	my	theirs	thy
him				ye

SPARE

As well as being marvelously beheadable *–spare/ pare/are/re/e* — and curtailable — *spare/spar/spa* — *spare* is the most anagrammable of all English words. Juggle *spare* and you get *apers, pares, parse, pears, rapes, reaps,* and *spear,* along with the rarer *apres, asper, prase,* and *presa.*

TARMAC

A number of four-letter words become new words when, contemporaneously, the front letter is looped to the back and the back to the front, among them *brag/grab*, *doom/mood*, *drop/prod*, *grip/prig*, *lair/rail*, *leap/peal*, and *part/tarp*. The first and last letters must be different, of course, and the result of this double loop is that the first and last letters are exchanged.

Rarer five-letter examples include *doper/roped*, *khans/shank*, *lever/revel*, *robes/sober*, and *sinew/wines*.

Reaching for six-letter prizes, we note the pattern *dapper/rapped*, *dipper/ripped*, and *dubber/rubbed*. More elegantly, *tarmac/car mat* features a sense of semantic kinship. It's a shame that *car mat* is two words.

TEMP

The best of "pseudo-comparatives" — words that can add both an *-er* and *-est* but that don't relate at all to true comparisons of adjectives. That is, the triad of *temp/temper/tempest* looks like the *small/smaller/smallest* adjective model, but it isn't a true progression of adjectives. Other examples: *be/beer/beest*; *p/per/pest*. Pry/prior/priest and *mole/molar/molest* come so close, except that their comparative forms lack the crucial *-er* "suffix." *Deter-detest* is the ultimate heartbreaker — a comparative and a superlative, but with no baseword.

THEREIN

Lurking in *therein* are ten words with letters adjacent and in order:

ere	her	herein	re	the
he	here	in	rein	there

UNITED

In an installment of Johnny Hart's comic strip *B.C.,* one caveman screams at another, "No, no, no, no! I distinctly said to *gird* your *loins!*" The other caveguy has drawn a grid on a lion. The humor of this episode arises from the fact that a number of words

transform into other words when two adjacent letters are switched —
trial/trail, diary/dairy, silver/sliver, closets/closest, infraction/infarction, and, of
course *gird/grid* and *loins/lions.*

With the same interchange of neighboring letters, *united* becomes its
opposite — *untied. Complaint* and *compliant* form near opposites, as do
sacred and *scared.* Depending on your point of view, *marital* and *martial* may
be antonyms or synonyms.

USHERS

Has there ever been a word like *ushers?* Within the house of *ushers* dwell
almost all of humankind — five pronouns, with letters adjacent and in
sequence: *he, her, hers, she,* and *us.*

George Canning (1770-1828) was a British statesman and for a brief time Prime Minister of England. Along the way, he created one of the most famous of all word puzzles:

> A word there is of plural number,
> Foe to ease and tranquil slumber.
> Any other word you take
> And add an *s* will plural make,

THE MIDWAY

> But if you add an *s* to this,
> So strange the metamorphosis:
> Plural is plural now no more
> And sweet what bitter was before.

The word is *cares,* which, with the addition of a second *s,* becomes *caress.*

The Girl's Own Paper (1881) contained a puzzle about hidden animals, animal names that are camouflaged because their letters, though in order and consecutive, are distributed through more than one word. Flush a hidden animal from each of the following sentences and two from the last:

> Impossible! O, pardon me, by no means.
> The lamb is one of my pets.
> At last a girl moved.
> He made errors on purpose.
> I must give it up, I grieve to say.
> Well, I only got terrified out of my wits.

And the hidden animals are . . . *leopard, bison, stag, deer, pig,* and *lion* and *otter.*

Ladies and gentlemen! Boys and girls! Gamesters of all ages! Before you leave the Word Circus, may I have your attention one last time?

Step right up and roll or hurl the ball into the hole! Knock the dolls off the shelf! Flip the ring around the bottleneck! Shoot your beebees — or any other letters — at the sitting ducks! Hammer the platform and drive the metal up the pole so that your strength will ring a bell! Direct the dart into the balloons to uncover the hidden booty! Please listen to this pitchman. He can make you rich, man.

As Sherlock Holmes says in "The Abby Grange," "Come, Watson, come! The game is afoot." And as Shakespeare's huntsman in *King Henry VI* explains, "This way, my lord, for this way lies the game." Enter the midway of games and win a prize with each enterprise. Show your skill as an alphabetamaniac, letterophile, wordaholic, logolept, and verbivore by playing some letter-perfect games of skill. All of the answers await you at the end of the midway.

HE MADE ERRORS ON ~~THE~~ PURPOSE.

244 • the midway

LETTER WORDS

Each of the following definitions yields a word that sounds just like a letter of the alphabet. Fill in each blank with the proper letter and then string the letters together to reveal the hidden message. If all your answers are correct, you'll reap a rich reward.

1. a honey of an insect; exist
2. vision organ; pronoun
3. exclamation
4. a blue and white bird
5. indefinite article
6. large body of water; perceive
7. woman's name
8. green vegetable
9. to be in debt; exclamation
10. beverage; golf peg

BIG-NAME GRAMMAGRAMS

Each clue below yields a proper name consisting entirely of letter sounds. The number of letters sounded in each name is represented by the parenthesized number.

1. He struck out. (2)
2. She's a contented cow. (2)
3. Garfield's canine stooge. (2)
4. He led Shaw's band. (2)
5. Today she's a morning show hostess. (2)
6. He courted an Irish Rose. (2)
7. He franchises roast beef. (2)
8. This poet could not stop for death. (3)

CALLING ON THE HOMOPHONE

Each of the following clues should lead you to an answer involving two homophones. For example an "ostracized poet" is a *barred bard*. The answers to the first fifteen are all single syllable words, and the answers to the second fifteen are composed of polysyllabic words.

1. wan bucket
2. perceives the deep waters
3. dungarees for chromosomes
4. levy on push nails
5. unadorned airliner
6. forbidden musical group
7. rapier flew
8. tube to wash garden tools
9. uninterested plank
10. to inveigle soft drinks
11. spun globe
12. visitor estimated
13. large frame
14. villainous singer
15. octet consumed food
16. evil armed force
17. change the worship platform
18. young digger

(SCANDINAVIAN ENDING)

19. braver rock
20. fearful man quivered
21. inactive false god
22. more skillful wagerer
23. Scandinavian ending
24. boarder gossip

25. sedentary writing paper
26. military belly button
27. gathered the condiment
28. convalescent's forbearance
29. renter's boundary
30. mansion's etiquette

A HYMN TO HETERONYMS

In the following poem, fill in each of the eight pairs of blanks with a heteronym. The number of letters missing in each heteronymic answer is indicated by the number of dotted lines:

Why d_ _s the prancing of so many d_ _s
   Explain why down d_ _ _e the white d_ _ _e,
Or why p_ _ _y cat has a p_ _ _y old sore
   And b_ _ s sing b_ _ s notes of their love?

_ _ they always sing, "_ _ re mi" and stare, ag_ _ _,
   At eros, ag_ _ _ each m_ _ _ _ _e?
Their love's not m_ _ _ _ _e; there's an over_ _ _ of love.
   Even over_ _ _ fish are quite with it.

These bass fish have never been in short s_ _ _ _y
   As they s_ _ _ _y spawn without waiting.
With their love fluids bubbling, abundant, s_ _ _ _ _ive,
   There's many a s_ _ _ _ _ive mating.

AN ANAGRAMMATICAL RIDDLE

What do the following words have in common?: *thorn, shout, seat/sate, stew/wets.*

A BIRD'S I VIEW

All birds have two eyes. Name two four-letter birds that have two *i*s.
Add an *i* to *petrel*, anagram the letters, and you'll come up with a *reptile.*

Add an *i* to each of the following birds, anagram the letters, and what new words will you generate?:

gander ostrich parrot raven toucan

ANAGRAMARAMA

In each of the following phrases, change either the first or last word to an anagram of the other half. In each case, the new word will be a synonym of the base word or words. For example, in the phrase "autographed the design," you would change the first word to *signed* to produce "signed the design"; similarly, the phrase "Socratic word puzzle" would become "Socratic acrostic."

1. pilot's firearm
2. perceives section
3. mother's container
4. lauded diapers
5. incautious runway
6. talented fidget
7. hurry, sleuth
8. gamester's parsley
9. most joyful epitaphs
10. sectional shore
11. remember the cellar
12. resist sibling
13. viewing genies
14. married devotee
15. hope to praise
16. resign, crooner
17. leather North Carolinian
18. entrap father
19. generate an adolescent
20. grounded long shot

21. license for muteness
22. aboard far away
23. brides in rubble
24. diminutive Batman
25. hides rubies

26. singer's entrance
27. vainest residents
28. Congressional treason
29. Congressional rationales
30. grandest police traps

REMEMBER THE CELLAR!

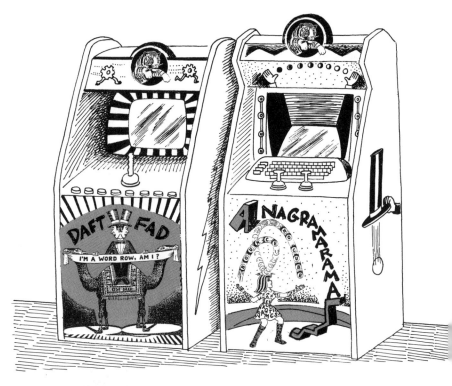

SERAPH PHRASE

What single word yields all of the following aptagrams?: I'M TRADE'S EVENTS; ITEMS AT VENDERS; TRADES VEST IN 'EM; VAST MERIT'S NEED.

DAFT FAD

Identify each two-word palindromic phrase defined below. To arrive at each palindrome use one word in each clue and a synonym for the other word or words. Thus, "wooden crib" would be *birch crib*.

1. speedy car
2. angry dam
3. my exercise room
4. regal beer
5. canine god
6. maritime van

7. snoopy son
8. gloomy doom
9. Caregivers run.
10. Party concealed explosive
11. Superiors sob.
12. Don't start snoozing.
13. guru carpet
14. evil martini fruit
15. bold toss
16. lost sun
17. sinful aroma
18. shrimp warp
19. gave back diaper
20. food cans
21. dog coop
22. Experts know.
23. trusty nailer
24. Nevada boner
25. Party ever!
26. dig up denim
27. solo escorts
28. standard cots
29. straw eruptions
30. Late? Drat!
31. We thread.
32. No more pots.
33. barge robbery
34. personal journal raid
35. Binge on grog.
36. killed rum
37. head tap
38. hermit's ulcer
39. Take a chance, sir!
40. Some documents

STRAW ERUPTIONS

HALF AND HALF

Below are twenty words, each three letters in length. Combine each word in the left-hand column with another in the right-hand column so as to make ten six-letter words. Each three-letter word must be used only once. Example: *tar* + *get* = *target*

bud		age
car		air
fat		den
gob		get
imp		her
man		ice
not		ire
sat		let
war		pet
win		try

Now the game becomes a little harder. This time, the twenty three-letter words are simply listed in alphabetical order. For each of the ten answers, you are to yoke together *any* two of the words below so as to make ten six-letter words. Again, be sure that you don't use any item more than once:

ace	one
ale	ore
ant	pal
ash	per
beg	put
end	rid
fin	sea
ham	see
hem	son
leg	the

Now let's step up to some four-plus-four = eight-letter words. Again, the four-letter words that combine to create the ten eight-letter words appear alphabetically. You are invited to restore the original words, using any two sets of four letters. Example: *lace* + *rate* = *lacerate*.

bard	mars
bell	mist
city	owed
come	rain
dies	rate
disc	rest
gene	rust
gram	scab
king	scar
lose	thin

MULTIPLE CHARADES

Here are ten long words stitched together from three or more shorter words. Each component is briefly defined and the number of letters in each part indicated in parentheses. Example: honey (4) + bird (3) + Noah's boat (3) = *meadowlark*.

1. opinion sample (4) + preposition (2) + devoured (3)
2. thus (2) + cat sound (3) + this place (4)
3. ghetto (4) + exist (2) + band (4)
4. thong (4) + auto (3) + country (6)
5. gremlin (3) + conjunction (2) + song (4)
6. donkey (3) + donkey (3) + preposition (2) + consumed (3)
7. store of money (4) + ending to prayer (4) + to count (5)
8. cauto (3) + writing instrument (3) + attempt (3)
9. preposition (2) + length of time (4) + pronoun (2) + canvas shelter (4)
10. thin circle (4) + outer edge (3) + preposition (2) + preposition (2) + charged subatomic particle (3)

OFF WITH THEIR HEADS!

Try to solve these time-honored beheadment riddles:

> My whole often stands on one leg.
> If you behead me, I stand on two.
> Behead me again, and I stand upon four.

* * *

> Take one letter from me, and I slay.
> Take away two, and I may die,
> If my whole does not save me.

The answers are *glass/lass/ass* and *skill/kill/ill*.

By removing an initial letter, then a second initial letter, list the words that correspond to the following synonyms. For example, the clue "yell (6), best part, measure" yields *scream/cream/ream.* The parenthesized numbers indicate the length of each baseword.

1. tendency (5), tear apart, conclude
2. frown angrily (5), monk's hood, bird
3. rubbish (5), foolhardy, residue
4. tiny seed (5), skin opening, raw mineral, in reference to
5. use or deplete (5), in abeyance, finish
6. gulp down (7), slop around, permit
7. brave (5), pester, away
8. location (5), fabric, expert
9. unchanging (6), furniture, competent
10. slant (5), frisk, song, yes
11. sermonize (6), range, every
12. basket (5), spool, fish
13. backsliding (7), pass, mistake, part of a church
14. placed (6), dragged, indebted, married
15. oriental (7), behind, severe, bird
16. spite (6), Carroll's heroine, insects, frozen water
17. woman (5), first man, barrier, is
18. increasing (7), propelling, in debt, pinion
19. defraud (5), warmth, consume, preposition
20. females (5), portent, males

NEXT?

What is the next letter in each of the following series?:

1. OTTFFSS
2. FSTFF
3. JFMAMJJ
4. SSMTWT
5. WAJMMAJ

FIRST ADDITION

The opposite of a beheadment and curtailment is the adding of a letter to the front or back of a baseword. In a few instances, a one-syllable word can triple the total of its syllables:

1. Add the letter *a* to the beginning of a four-letter word that means "a charge upon a debt" to create a three-syllable word.
2. Add the letter *a* to the end of a three-letter word that means "exist" to make it three syllables.
3. Add the letter *o* to the end of a four-letter word that means "arrived" to make it three syllables.
4. Add the letter *o* to the end of a four-letter word that means "traveled" to make it three syllables.
5. Add the letter *i* after the first letter of a five-letter word that means "grin" to make it a three-syllable word.

KANGAROO COUNTRY

Name a country whose name means "East Land" that reposes as a joey in the name of another country whose name, in a different language, means "South Land." When you arrive at a solution, you'll discover that this has truly been a kangaroo challenge.

KANGAROO SPORTS CHALLENGE

Name four teams in professional basketball, baseball, football, and ice hockey that each conceal a second professional team as a joey. Use the team name, not the city — *Cowboys,* for example.

WORD LADDERS

Change the first word into the second word by changing one letter at a time in the number of steps indicated by the parenthesized number:

1. SIN to WOE (3)
2. LEAD to GOLD (3)
3. TRY to WIN (4)
4. LESS to MORE (4)
5. SHIP to SAIL (4)
6. DOZE to WAKE (5)

7. HEAT to FIRE (5)   9. LION to BEAR (5)
8. PIG to STY (5)   10. HAND to FOOT (5)

GAG ME WITH A SPOONERISM

Finish the set-up story by completing the spoonerized *punch* line:

An ancient jungle king tyrannized his subjects and forced them to build one elaborate throne after another. First, they constructed a throne of mud, then bamboo, then tin, then copper, then silver, and so on. When the monarch grew tired of each throne, he would store it in the attic of his grass hut. One day the attic collapsed, and the thrones crashed down upon the chief's head and killed him.

The moral of the tale is: People who live in grass houses _____ _____ _____.

SILVER SPOONERISMS

In each couplet in the following rhyme, the first line ends with a word pair that is spoonerized in the next line. Fill in the blanks with the missing words, using the number of dotted lines as clues to the number of letters. Tip: The first letter(s) of each endword indicates the first letter(s) of each missing word.

When Sandy sees a _ _ _ing crow,
It makes her weep. The _ _ _ing flow

Runs down her nose and _ _ _ _ and cheeks
Into a cup that _ _ _ _ _ and leaks.

Sometimes her makeup's _ _ _ _ow hue
Just smears when she shouts, "_ _ _ _ _, you!"

She gobbles up the _ _ _ _ _ beans,
Which overflow her _ _ _ _, jeans,

And all. She keeps on _ _ _ _ing weight.
(It shows up in her _ _ _ing gait.)

"I laugh a lot," she _ _ _ _ _ _ _ _ now,
While munching on pig's _ _ _ _ _ _ _ _ chow.

Which proves I've made a _ _ _den rule
Of eating all the _ _den gruel."

LETTERS ARE FOREVER

In each list that follows, a parade of letters marches in alphabetical order. What do the letters in each line have in common? For the first section, what aspect of design accounts for the unity?:

    1. AEFHIKLMNTVWXYZ
    2. abcdefghjmnopqrstu

3. bdfhijklt

4. *fgjpqyz*

5. AHIMOTUVWXY

6. BCDEHIKOX

7. HINOSXZ

8. EMW

What concept other than shape unites each of the following groupings?:

9. BCDFGHJKLMNPQRSTVXZ

10. CDILMVX

11. AJKQ

12. ABCGIJKOPQRTUY

13. ABCDEFGHIJKLMNOPRSTUVWXY

14. EIOPQRTUWY

15. ADEHLNIORSTU

STRINGS ATTACHED

In a continuing effort to improve upon the frustrating *gry* puzzle, the Word Circus presents ten superior puzzles of the *gry* type:

1. What four-letter word ends in *eny?*
2. Three common English words contain the letter sequence *shion. Fashion* and *cushion* are two of them. What is the third word?
3. *Nervous, grievous,* and *mischievous* end in *vous.* Identify a fourth word with the same ending.
4. *Manse* is not a very common word these days, but two common, uncapitalized English words also end in *anse.* Name them.
5. *Suspicion* and *coercion* end in *cion.* Identify a third such word.
6. What verb ends in *dict* but doesn't rhyme with *predict, contradict,* and *interdict?*
7. What words end with each of the following letter strings (one word for each combination)?:

sede   *mt*   *inse*   *onse*

8. What words contain the following letter strings?:
    chsi   *chion*   *gnty*   *uia*
9. What words (one for each) contain a silent *ps* and *ch?*
10. List four words that begin with *dw.*

RE-VIEWING THE CIRCUS

Within each five-word set lurks a common denominator, a characteristic shared by every word in the cluster. Identify each characteristic. Example: In the set *deified, noon, pep,* and *sees,* all the words are palindromic.

1. deer, dog, gnat, ram, rat
2. dissident, hosannas, millimeter, sniffing, suffuse
3. category, crowned, dogma, emulate, wrench
4. blotter, escrow, forebear, scallion, vamoose
5. calmness, hijack, indefinite, stuck, worst
6. area, example, Israeli, onto, Urdu
7. gypsy, myrrh, nth, pygmy, rhythms
8. ambidextrous, cauliflower, exhaustion, housemaid, pandemonium
9. giggling, maharaja, possess, razzmatazz, whippersnapper
10. bassoon, coffee, raccoon, roommate, tattoo
11. are, eye, pea, queue, why
12. ewe, eye, hour, there, wee
13. id, shed, shell, wed, well
14. barbaric, bringing, counterterrorism, possessed, ratcatcher
15. civic, civil, livid, mimic, vivid
16. selective, sexist, slake, stern, swindles
17. ant, asp, manatee, mite, owl
18. chatter, frightful, revolution, treason, vindicate
19. peppery, pretty, quieter, rupture, typewriter
20. circus, cook, judge, solstice, zebras

As Belarius in *Cymbeline* exclaims, "The game is up!" So now we offer you a complete set of answers. If many of your responses match what you are about to read, snag yourself a blue ribbin' or a QP doll.

ANSWERS

LETTER WORDS: BIG JACKPOT

BIG-NAME GRAMMAGRAMS: 1. Casey (KC) 2. Elsie (LC) 3. Odie (OD) 4. Artie (RT) 5. Katie (KT) (Couric) 6. Abie (AB) 7. Arby (RB) 8. Emily (MLE) (Dickinson)

CALLING ON THE HOMOPHONE: 1. pale pail 2. sees seas 3. jeans genes 4. tacks tax 5. plain plane 6. banned band 7. sword soared 8. hoes hose 9. bored board 10. coax Cokes

11. whirled world 12. guest guessed 13. great grate 14. base bass 15. eight ate 16. malicious militias 17. alter altar 18. minor miner 19. bolder boulder 20. coward cowered

21. idle idol 22. better bettor 23. Finnish finish 24. roomer rumor 25. stationary stationery 26. naval navel 27. mustered mustard 28. patient's patience 29. boarder's border 30. manor's manners

BORED
BOARD

A HYMN TO HETERONYMS: does, dove, pussy, bass, do, agape, minute, overage, supply, secretive

AN ANAGRAMMATICAL RIDDLE: They are anagrams of the words *north, south, east,* and *west.*

A BIRD'S I VIEW: ibis, kiwi; grained or reading; historic; airport; ravine; auction.

ANAGRAMARAMA: 1. pilot's pistol 2. notices section 3. mother's thermos 4. praised diapers 5. unwary runway 6. gifted fidget 7. hustle, sleuth 8. player's parsley 9. happiest epitaphs 10. sectional coastline
11. recall the cellar 12. resist sister 13. seeing genies 14. married admirer 15. aspire to praise 16. resign, singer 17. leather tarheel 18. entrap parent 19. generate a teenager 20. grounded underdog
21. license for silence 22. aboard abroad 23. brides in debris 24. bantam Batman 25. buries rubies 26. singer's ingress 27. vainest natives 28. senator treason 29. senatorial rationales 30. grandest dragnets

SERAPH PHRASE: advertisements

DAFT FAD: 1. race car 2. mad dam 3. my gym 4. regal lager 5. dog god 6. navy van 7. nosy son 8. moody doom 9. nurses run 10. party boobytrap

11. Bosses sob. 12. Don't nod. 13. guru rug 14. evil olive 15. bold lob 16. lost sol 17. amoral aroma 18. prawn warp 19. repaid diaper 20. snack cans

21. pooch coop 22. Wonks know. 23. reliant nailer 24. Reno boner 25. Revel ever! 26. mine denim 27. solo gigolos 28. stock cots 29. straw warts 30. Tardy? Drat!

31. We sew. 32. Stop pots. 33. barge grab 34. diary raid 35. Gorge grog. 36. murdered rum 37. Pate tap 38. recluse's ulcer 39. Risk, sir! 40. some memos

HALF AND HALF:

I. budget, carpet, father, goblet, impair, manage, notice, satire, warden, wintry

II. anthem, ashore, begone, finale, hamper, legend, palace, putrid, season, seethe

III. bellowed, comedies, disclose, generate, grammars, mistrust, restrain, scabbard, scarcity, thinking

MULTIPLE CHARADES: 1. pollinate 2. somewhere 3. slumbering 4. reincarnate 5. importune 6. assassinate 7. fundamentally 8. carpentry 9. intermittent 10. discrimination

SPORE !

OFF WITH THEIR HEADS!: 1. trend 2. scowl 3. trash 4. spore 5. spend 6. swallow 7. stout 8. place 9. stable 10. splay 11. preach 12. creel 13. relapse 14. stowed 15. eastern 16. malice 17. madam 18. growing 19. cheat 20. women

NEXT?: 1. E (initials of cardinal numbers starting with *one*) 2. S (initials of ordinal numbers starting with *first*) 3. A (initials of months of the year) 4. F (initials of days of the week) 5. V (initials of presidential surnames; Van Buren is next)

FIRST ADDITIONS: 1. lien/alien 2. are/area 3. came/cameo 4. rode/rodeo 5. smile/simile

KANGAROO COUNTRY: *Austria/Australia*

KANGAROO SPORTS CHALLENGE: Packers/Pacers, Supersonics/Suns, Nuggets/Nets, Red Wings/Reds. Islanders also contains Reds, but backwards. Until recently, Bullets/Bulls would also have qualified, but the Washington NBA franchise is now called the Wizards. Pirates or Panthers/Pats does not count because Pats is a clipping of Patriots.

WORD LADDERS: Suggested answers (other chains are possible):

1. SIN-son-won-WOE (a quick journey!) 2. LEAD-load-goad-GOLD 3. TRY-wry-way-wan-WIN 4. LESS-loss-lose-lore-MORE 5. SHIP-skip-skid-said-SAIL 6. DOZE-dome-dame-lame-lake-WAKE 7. HEAT-head-herd-here-hire-FIRE 8. PIG-wig-wag-sag-say-STY 9. LION-loon-boon-boor-boar-BEAR 10. HAND-band-bond-fond-food-FOOT

GAG ME WITH A SPOONERISM: People who live in grass houses shouldn't stow thrones.

SILVER SPOONERISMS: flying crow/crying flow; lips and cheeks/chips and leaks; yellow hue/Hello, you; jelly beans/belly, jeans; gaining weight/waning gait; chuckles now/knuckles chow; golden rule/olden gruel

LETTERS ARE FOREVER: 1. All letters are made with straight lines 2. Made with curved lines 3. Above-the-line ascenders 4. Below-the-line descenders 5. Vertical symmetry

6. Horizontal symmetry 7. Each letter is the same when turned upside down 8. Letters made with four straight lines 9. Consonants, excluding *y* and *w* (which are sometimes used as vowels) 10. Roman numerals

11. Each letter appears on playing cards 12. Each letter sounds the same as a full word: *a, bee, see/sea, gee, eye/I/aye, jay, quay, o/oh, pea/pee, queue/cue, are, tea/tee, ewe/yew/you, why.* 13. Letters on a telephone dial 14. First row of letters on a standard *qwerty* keyboard 15. The thirteen letters that appear most frequently in writing. Frequency lists vary, but a typical one gives the order as ETAOINSHRDLU. (The first seven letters of this list are an anagram of *Estonia,* the native country of my daughter-in-law Triinu.)

STRINGS ATTACHED: 1. deny (*Eeny,* as in "eeny meeny miney moe," is not listed in most dictionaries.) 2. parishioner 3. rendezvous 4. expanse, cleanse 5. scion

6. indict 7. supersede, dreamt, rinse, response 8. fuchsia, stanchion, sovereignty, colloquial (also Algonquian and alleluia) 9. corps, yacht/fuchsia 10. dwarf(s), dweeb(s), dwell(ed/ing), dwindle(d/ing)

RE-VIEWING THE CIRCUS: 1. names of animals that can be reversed to spell other words 2. words in which is embedded a six-letter palindrome 3. words that begin with animal names 4. words that end with animal names 5. words containing three adjacent alphabetical letters in order

6. words that begin and end with the same vowel 7. words bereft of any of the major vowels 8. words containing all five of the major vowels 9. words that contain four instances of one letter 10. words with two touching sets of double letters

11. homophones of letters 12. homophones of pronouns 13. words that become contractions of pronouns when an apostrophe is inserted 14. words featuring adjacent pairs of triple letters 15. words that, when capitalized, consist entirely of Roman numerals

16. words that become new words when the initial *s* is looped to the back 17. animal names that become new words when the last letter is looped to the front 18. words that become new words with beheadment 19. words formed entirely from letters on the top letter row of a *qwerty* keyboard 20. words that begin and end with the same consonant sound spelled with different letters

AFTER

Life is a circus where thousands throng but none can stay. The only permanence of the circus is its impermanence. Each time the Greatest Show on Earth leaves a city, it tears itself down and piles itself onto railroad cars. Not so with the Word Circus.

Nothing now to mark the spot
But a littered vacant lot.
Sawdust in a heap, and where
The center ring stood, grass worn bare.

But remains the alphabet,
Ready to leap and pirouette.
May the spangled letters soar
In your head forever more.

WORD

Notes

Order of the performances: In the arrangement of the circus acts and attractions in this book there is method in the madness, as well as madness in the method.

After the barker barks us into the Big Top, into the ring rolls "The Bandwagon," in which letters themselves are spotlighted and the letter play must be heard to be fully appreciated. The bandwagon sets the stage for the two most famous acts of letter play — anagrams and palindromes. Palindromic words and statements can be thought of as a special kind of anagram in which the rearrangement of letters in the second half of the word or statement can be only one way — backwards. "Big-Name Acts" then exhibits the work that has been done anagramming and palindroming proper and generally famous names.

"Clown Cars" begins with charade words, which are close kin to palindromes. That is, unless the words in the palindromic statement are each self-contained, as in ABLE WAS I ERE I SAW ELBA, the letters in the second half must be read charadefully, but in reverse order. For example:

I'M A WORD
?I MA, WOR

"Clown Cars" introduces the concept of words hiding within words. In this particular act, the larger words — charade words, binades, and trinades — are composed entirely of smaller words, with nothing left over. The whole is the sum of its parts.

The next two chapters extend the phenomenon of words lurking within words. "The Shrinking Spotlight" shines upon deletions — beheadments, curtailments, and acrostics — larger words that become smaller words when certain letters are removed. "Kangaroo Words" constitute one especially lively member of this category in that letters are removed from various locations in the parent words to produce synonymous joeys that retain letter order.

Just as the previous chapters spotlighted the ability of words to become other words, "The Acro Bat" shows off letter clusters that fly through the air and in the process change from one word to another. But now the process is letter substitution, rather than charading, beheading, curtailing, or transdeleting.

"Words on a Wire" features words that tread narrow tightropes. The fun comes from the challenging restrictions placed upon the word-making materials or the spaces into which the letters can be compacted. This is also the spirit of "Mary Had a Letter Lamb," which reviews many of the circus acts in this book through variations on one poetic theme.

"A Letter-Perfect Sideshow" exhibits an array of logological categories beyond those already presented. This is an opportunity to show off some of the more bizarre words that cavort through that endless entertainment we call the English language.

Finally, just as some circusgoers enjoy playing games outside the tent, some readers of this book will have fun with the challenges that await them on "The Midway." Like "Mary Had a Letter Lamb," this final chapter, in a gaming format, acts as a review of the various attractions that have pounced and bounced and flounced and jounced around the Big Top.

What is letter play? (Part I) Throughout *The Word Circus,* I have striven mightily to avoid miscegenating morphemes (meaning-bearing units) with letter units. My view is that when morphological manipulation starts, pure logology ends.

I'll illustrate with a few exhibits:

*The anagrammatical looping of multiple letters, such as the pairs *bedlam/lambed* and *stable/ablest,* is far more logologically satisfying than the looping of *songbird/birdsong* and *takeover/overtake* because logology is about letter play, not the syntactic rearrangement of morphemic (meaning-bearing) units.

*In five instances that I have identified, the reversing of two parts of a compound word yields a meaning opposite to that of the original compound — *upset* (overturn)/*set up* (assemble); *overlook* (ignore)/*look over* (peruse); *uphold* (support)/*hold up* (hinder); *overcome* (conquer)/*come over* (surrender); *withstand* (resist)/*stand with* (join). But again, such reversals involve the interchange of morphemes rather than letter patterns that are not tied to meaning.

*Logologists know their *s* from a hole in the ground. The curtailing of terminal *s*'s in plural nouns or third-person singular verbs — *words/word, speaks/speak* — draws a yawn. The looping of an initial *s*, as in *scar/cars, speak/peaks,* inspires a burst of apathy. Why? Because the *s* is primarily a meaning-bearing element.

* *Partially/partly* is not worth discussing as a kangaroo family because etymology dominates letter pattern. *Contaminate/taint* is a star pairing because the letter play's the thing. The banishing of internal solids — as*sur*ed, en*joy*ment, in*toxic*ated — from the species of joeys is somewhat tied to the fact that such solids usually house meaning.

*The charades *housecat* = *house* + *cat* and *peacock* = *pea* + *cock* do not excite the lover of letter play. *Antelope* = *ant* + *elope* and *pigeon* = *pig* + *eon* do because the charade components are marvelous accidents.

*Bookend words of the type *ligament* = *lint* + *game* work better than the type *departed* = *part* + *deed* because the bookends in the second class are essentially morphological, hence second class.

*Both *jumbo shrimp* and *Connecticut* = *connect* + *I cut* are oxymorons, but the second example boasts the added feature of sheer accidence of letters.

* *Widower* is the only common word in English in which the masculine form is derived from the feminine base. Interesting, but the *-er* is primarily morphological, not logological.

The star of the Word Circus is logology (the realm of letter engineering), not morphology (the realm of meaning-bearing units). Those who frequent the Word Circus are not morpheme addicts. If relevant meanings accompany letter play, those meanings are results of the letter play. When I say that "the letter play's the thing," I mean that the letter play comes first.

Did I use a computer to gather the words for this circus? I'm glad I asked me that. The answer is not at all, except to word process the manuscript. I always prefer artifice intelligence to artificial intelligence.

I. The Bandwagon

With cultivated scholarship, fertile wit, and down-to-earth common sense, I make a modest attempt to turn the vast and unweeded terrain of word-cluster classification into a manageable garden of delight.

To begin, jettison the term *homonym* — and if you've never heard of or read it before, pretend that I never mentioned it here. *Homonym,* you see, has started to resemble the word *love.* We modern English speakers love our parents and children; we love our spouses and paramours. We love our country; we love country music. We love God; we love our new shoes. We love *The Iliad;* we love *Love Story.*

Like the word *love, homonym* has become a do-it-all-purpose convenience label that signifies all manner of word pairs, including the types that I'm about to cover. Whatever sound and fury *homonym* may have once possessed now signifies nothing.

Instead, employ the following labels:

Homographs: two or more words that are written alike and sound alike but have different meanings. Sometimes the words will share derivational DNA: *plot* (storyline), *plot* (a small area of ground), and *plot* (a secret plan) are the same word with different meanings (polysemy). Sometimes the words will be etymologically unrelated. *Bat* (mammal) and *bat* (wooden implement for hitting a ball) and *mint* (aromatic plant) and *mint* (place where money is manufactured) share no common ancestry.

Homophones: two or more words that sound alike but are spelled differently and have different meanings, as *bare bear* and "A three-*toed toad towed* a load." To call these phonetic clusters *homonyms* is to invite taxonomic chaos. The classical word parts of *homograph* and *homophone* clearly signify "same writing" and "same sound" respectively.

Heteronyms: pairs of words with the same spelling but different pronunciations, meanings, and derivations. Among the best of these are *entrance* (opening) and *entrance* (beguile) and *moped* (motorbike) and *moped* (sulked).

Incredibly, the grammagram crossword puzzle gimmick works also in French!:

Across	Down
1. Que font les moustiques	1. aime (loves)
2. Que font les chiens	2. au (water)
3. Que font les serpentes	3. air (air)
4. Que font les dentes	4. de (thimble)

1 M	2 O	3 R	4 D
2 M	O	R	D
3 M	O	R	D
4 M	O	R	D

We can add the following words, many of them unusual, to the triple homophones list: *ait* (island), *ate, eight; baize* (coarse fabric) *bays, beys* (Turkish provincial governors); *bight* (bend in a coast), *bite, byte; bird, burd* (maiden), *burred* (characterized by burs); *censer* (dispenser of incense), *censor, sensor; cinque* (five), *sink, sync* (informal for *synchronization*); *crews, cruise, cruse* (small vessel); *earn, erne* (sea eagle), *urn; fane* (church), *fain* (happy), *feign; fays* (elves, faiths), *faze, phase; fraise* (fortification), *frays, phrase; gored, gourd, gourde* (monetary unit of Haiti); *knap* (to break with a quick blow), *nap, nappe* (sheet); *lacks, lacs* (resinous substances), *lax; lay, lea* (tract of open ground), *lei; lea* (alternate pronunciation), *lee, li* (music term); *mean, mesne* (intermediate), *mien* (demeanor); *marc* (fruit residue) *mark, marque* (a brand); *sewn, sone* (measurement of sound), *sown; sign, sine, syne* (since); slew, slough, slue (to swing around); *stade* (stadium), *staid, stayed; steal, steel, stele* (part of a vascular plant); *stoop, stoup* (beverage container), *stupe* (hot, wet cloth); *tael* (Chinese unit of value), *tail, tale.*

Additional quadruples: *birr* (force, energy, vigor) makes *brr/bur/burr* a quadruple; *cense* (incense) makes *cents/scents/sense* a quadruple; *heigh* (exclamation) makes *hi/hie/high* a quadruple; *lays, laze, leas* (tracts of open ground), *leis; pallette* (armor plate) makes *palate/pallet/palette* a quadruple; *pic* (picador's lance) makes *peak/peek/pique* a quadruple; *wheal* (welt) makes *weal/we'll/wheel* a quadruple; *weald* (wooded country), *whealed* (welted), *wheeled, wield.*

Carat/caret/carrot/karat constitute the only quadruple two-syllable homophone. *Are* (metric land measure) and *eyre* (English itinerant judge) make the *air/ere/err/heir* cluster the most homophonous of all, especially if we add the proper names *Ayer* and *Eyre.*

To the twenty-two spellings of *oh* in the sentence, we can add La Rouchefouc*auld,* Perr*ault,* f*aux* pas, *haut* monde, table d'*ho*te, b*oat*swain, Goun*od,* yo*l*k, de tr*op,* prev*ost.*

See Richard Lederer, "Orthograffiti," *Word Ways,* November 1978, and subsequent *Word Ways* "Colloquy" discussions for a list of more than twenty to more than thirty variations of the letters and letter combinations that generate the vowel sounds *ay, ee, eye, oh,* and *oo* and the consonant blend *sh.* See also "The Ultimate Homonym Group," *Word Ways,* November 1984, in which Dmitri Borgmann identifies eighty-four (!) different ways in which the sound *ee* is represented in English words and names.

Note the elegant pattern of the three heteronymic plurals from multiple singulars: The singular *axis* and the heteronymic plural *axes* (when it signifies the plural of *axe*) are homophones; the singular *basis* and the heteronymic plural *bases* (the plural of *base*) are homophones; and the singular *taxis* and the heteronymic plural *taxes* (the plural of *tax*) are also homophones. In other words, *axes, bases,* and *taxes* are each homophonic with a singular of which each is *not* the plural.

Additional heteronyms that require accents include *attachés, chargé, coupé, curé, exposé, lamé, maté, pliés, rosé, touchés,* and *visé.*

I have lived a capitonymic life. My mother, Leah Perry Lederer, was born in Reading (Pennsylvania), a capitonym, and, for thirty-five years, I resided in Concord (New Hampshire), another capitonym.

Capitonymic pairs that we perceive as English words — *Concord/concord, Polish/polish, Reading/reading* — are more satisfying than pairs that strike us as "foreign" — *Forget/forget, Nice/nice, Tangier/tangier.*

It should be noted that silent letters frequently gain a voice when the baseword is extended by a suffix:

B: bomb/bombard	*G:* resign/resignation	*N:* condemn/condemnation
C: muscle/muscular	*H:* vehicle/vehicular	*P:* receipt/recipient
E: line/linear	*I:* fruit/fruition	*U:* circuit/circuitous

II. Ana Gram the Juggler

The word *anagram* — Greek *ana,* "back," and *gramma,* "letter" — originally referred to a word or phrase that, when written backward, yielded a new word or phrase. Nowadays, we call such reversals *semordnilaps,* while *anagram* designates words or phrases produced by any rearrangement of letters, not just reversals.

Throughout this book, I have followed the basic rule laid down by William Drummond in his 1711 disquisition on the *Character of a Perfect Anagram:* "In an anagram there must not be fewer nor more nor other letters, but the same, and as many as in the name."

Ray Bradbury tells us that "creativity is constant surprise." That's why well-mixed anagrams, such as *maraschino/harmonicas* and *reclaim/miracle,* are inherently more pleasing than lightly shaken refreshments, such as *waddle/dawdle* and *however/whoever.*

I'll tuck the popular but politically incorrect *mother-in-law/* HITLER WOMAN (Nypho) into this section. These decisions are necessitated by a world in which poetry and politics often collide.

Some observers identify perfect anagrams as those that evidence at least as many transformations as there are letters in each word, but without the requirement that each letter must act as the lead letter. Examples include *pares/parse/pears/rapes/reaps/spare/spear* and *drapes/padres/parsed/rasped/spared/spread.*

Embedded in the dirtier and grittier stretches of the information superhighway are the anagrams ASPIRING WHORE OF HUMANITY and I'M ON A HUGE WISPY RHINO FART.

III. The Palindromedary

Alistair Reid expresses what may be the very heart of the fascination for matters palindromic: "The dream which occupies the tortuous mind of every palindromist is that somewhere within the confines of the language lurks the Great Palindrome, the nutshell which not only fulfills the intricate demands of the art, flowing sweetly in both directions, but which also contains the Final Truth of Things."

In the quirkily brilliant *I Love Me, Vol. I,* p. 262, Michael Donner explains perspicaciously that palindromania has "at last [been] correctly understood to be not a disorder at all but rather the heightened sense of order we now know it to be." I concur. I believe that in our species is evolving a heightened wonderment at and facility with the universe of letters.

In 1892, William Walsh stated in his *Hand-Book of Literary Curiosities:* "After centuries of endeavor, so few really good anagrams have been rolled down to us. One may assert that all of the superb anagrams now extant may be contained in a pillbox." Look at the field of logology since 1965, the year Borgmann's *Language on Vacation* was published and shortly before the birth of *Word Ways,* and compare this work with what came before. You'll see what I mean about our ineluctable rendezvous with logological destiny.

For another view of letter play, hark to the caveat of American poet James Merrill: "We speak wistfully of sounding the depths of language, but language has its shallows too, and we can drown in those just as easily as in the raptures of the former." I tell you, gentle reader, that, in making *The Word Circus,* I almost did drown in the shallows of language. Letters beguiled me with their siren song, and, like Narcissus, I gazed and gaped and gawked at myself, from shore to shallows and back again. What saved me from plummeting forever into my own image — into all those letters — was having to come up for air periodically to construct the poems and the narrative that became the context for the world of this book. "Till human voices wake us, and we drown."

At the same time, I'll state here that I absolutely loved making *The Word Circus*. Not enough emphasis is given to the fact that writing is an incredibly joyful way to learn. In writing an entire book about an area of language relatively new to me, I discovered what I did not know I knew.

Hallah, denned, and *debbed* are not familiar enough to be included in my list of six-letter palindromic words.

In *Word Ways,* February 1991, Doug Hoylman demonstrates how palindromes are built by inserting palindromic units within palindromic units:

SIT, OTIS.

SIT ON OTIS.

SIT ON A PAN, OTIS.

SIT ON A POTATO PAN OTIS.

SIT ON A POT ATOP A POTATO PAN, OTIS.

SIT ON A POT ATOP A ROD, A PAW, A JAR, A CAP, A TAG, A BAT, A MALL, A WAD, A WALL, A MAT, A BAG, A TAP, A CAR, A JAW, A PAD, OR A POTATO PAN, OTIS.

Whole-word palindromes, such as ABLE WAS I ERE I SAW ELBA, STEP ON NO PETS, and RATS LIVE ON NO EVIL STAR are relatively rare in the canon of logology. I agree with Borgmann, who says that such word-reversal statements are "really a sign of inferior craftsmanship, since almost anyone can juggle palindromic words and reversals around in almost mechanical fashion until a meaningful group of words emerges. . . . [W]hat requires genuine skill is the construction of a palindromic sentence which, read in reverse, has each word sliding over from one to another of the words used in the frontward reading." Such deficiencies did not deter the poet Anne Sexton from asking her daughter to promise that RATS LIVE ON NO EVIL STAR would be engraved on her tombstone.

In *I Love Me, Vol. I,* Donner observes, "Composing word-unit palindromes is an entirely different kettle of fish from composing letter-unit palindromes. . . . The word-unit composer seems to require as good a grasp of syntactic possibilities as the letter-unit composer requires of spelling possibilities. The only catch is that the two types of familiarity are quite distinct and perhaps equally hard to acquire."

I submit that it is because whole-word palindromes and word-reversal palindromes involve words, i.e. morphological units, that they occupy a lower stratum in the logological pantheon than do the more familiar kind of palindromic statement, which leaps the spaces separating words.

IV. Big-Name Acts

The publication of this book comes just before the Roman Palindromic Biennium. The years 1999 and 2000 in Roman numeral form are MIM and MM (both kangarooed in the word *millennium*). The most recent string of Roman palindromic years occurred II and III; MIM and MM mark the last time that palindromic years — Arabic or Roman — can occur consecutively. So, don't wait till 2002 to start your palindramatic celebration. You can start right now.

As we discover in "Words On a Wire," the letters *H* and *I* are also horizontally and vertically symmetrical. But the horizontal halves do not match the vertical halves in the manner of *O* and *X*. That's why the symmetry of OXO is especially fearful. That's why the OXO delivery trucks are emblazoned with OXOXOXOXOXOXOXOXOXOXOXOXO.

V. Clown Cars

Note that *shake spear* contains four vowels and six consonants.

VI. The Shrinking Spotlight

Consistent with our devotion to letter patterns rather than morphological units, the focus is on non-inflected words that become different words when deleted in some manner. *Electrohysterograph/y* curtails a much longer word than the other examples, but who cares?

The *glass/lass/ass* poem is closely related to the famous story about a professor who put up a notice that he would "meet my classes tomorrow." Some prankster beheaded *classes,* but the prof one-upped the student by beheading the baseword yet again.

Scoop/coop constitute another pair in which the beheadment doubles the syllable total — if one takes the beheaded word to be the heteronymic *co-op.* Similarly, *does/doe* could be added to the list of embedded animal names if one takes the heteronymic baseword to be the present tense of the verb *do.*

Sating changes both vowel sounds when curtailed: *sating/satin.*

VII. Kangaroo Words

Other examples of embedded words made up entirely of adjacent letters are ex*ist,* f*actual,* blot*ch,* be*late*d, pr*offer,* c*lump,* s*elect,* c*rude,* con*federated,* ab*errant,* and umptee*nth.*

A closely related corollary to Lederer's Law of Kangaroo Words is that mother and joey should not be etymologically related in an obvious way. Applying this ruling is a subjective procedure, but I believe that most logologists would find little pleasure in alternative versions of the same morpheme, as in *prim*ordi*al* and *prim*ev*al.* This corollary bars specimens such as *amica-ble, arm*aments, *circ*umambu*late, cleans*ed, *clos*ure, *contra*dicto*ry, defini*tive, *dis*em*bark, equi*tab*le, hyp*erbol*e, imag*in*ing, in*cap*ability, mar*ket, nest*led, oblig*ated, pant*aloon*s, plat*ter, prat*tle, revol*u*tion, sat*iate, spl*atter, spl*utter, techn*olog*ical,* and *trust*worth*y.*

In addition to the degree of etymological disparity and lexical synonymy, kangaroo-joey families grow in satisfaction according to the number of hops and the length of the joey. According to these criteria, among the most lively of marsupial pairs are: *deliberated/debated, fabrication/fiction, nourished/nursed, rambunctious/raucous, rapscallion/rascal,* and *supervisor/superior.* With an eleven-letter joey, *investigating/instigating* would certainly join the elite group, except that the synonymy is not quite up to the standards of the Word Circus management. Similarly, *masturbation/maturation* are not quite synonymic neighbors.

Supervisor/superior/prior comes tantalizingly close to qualifying as another three-generation kangaroo family. Alas, the *prior* is a bit too much of a stretch.

Vainglorious/valorous and *intimidate/intimate* scintillate among the anti-kangaroo families.

Joviality/jolity/joy come oh so close to constituting a fourth three-generation kangaroo family, but *jolity* is too archaic a spelling of *jollity* to qualify.

IX. Words on a Wire

What is letter play? (Part II) Something different seems to be going on in this chapter. In each of the preceding acts, the entertainment springs from a comparison — between a word or statement and its anagrammatical relative; between the first half of a palindromic word or statement and its self-reflecting second half; between a single word and its charaded constituents; between a kangaroo word and its synonymous joey; between the two words that form the top and bottom rung of a word ladder, a shiftgram, or a spoonerism; between a grammagram and its aural letter parts; between or among the siblings in a homophonic or capitonymic family.

In matters of abstemious words, pangrams, lipograms, univocalics, Roman numeral words, telephone words, typewriter words, and the like, the entertainment appears to repose in the tightrope patterns of those words. Perhaps, though, the thrill of such logological constructions thrums also in a comparative mode — between ordinary words, manufactured from a wide selection among our twenty-six letters, and words on a wire, woven from just a few strands.

The words *HAL* and *typewriter* have long been shrouded in misunderstanding:

In a 1992 *New York Times* interview, *2001* author Arthur C. Clarke explains that the relationship between *HAL* and *I.B.M.* was pure coincidence. "I've been trying to put that myth to rest for the past twenty years," said Clarke. In his *Acronymania,* page 182, Don Hauptman reveals that *HAL* really stands for "*h*euristically programmed *al*gorithmic computer."

While *HAL* turns out to be a coincidence, the presence of *typewriter* on a single typewriter row is less of a chance conjunction of the stars than meets the untelescoped eye. The *qwerty* keyboard was designed to slow typists down while allowing salepersons to type the word *typewriter* more facilely.

X. Mary Had a Letter Lamb

Here are more of Ross Eckler's lipogrammatical Marys.
With no *s:*

> Mary had a little lamb
>   With fleece a pale white hue,
> And everywhere that Mary went
>   The lamb kept in her view.
>
> To academe he went with her
>   (Illegal and quite rare).
> It made the children laugh and play
>   To view a lamb in there.

No *h:*

> Mary owned a little lamb;
>   Its fleece was pale as snow,
> And every place its mistress went
>   It certainly would go.
>
> It followed Mary to class one day
>   (It broke a rigid law).
> It made the students giggle aloud;
>   A lamb in class all saw.

No *t:*

> Mary had a pygmy lamb,
>   His fleece was pale as snow,
> And every place where Mary walked,
>   Her lamb did also go;

He came inside her classroom once
(Which broke a rigid rule).
How children all did laugh and play
On seeing lamb in school.

The most extensive paying of lipogram service in English is the 1939 novel *Gadsby*, by Ernest Vincent Wright, which contains 50,110 words — and not a single letter *e* — no love, no sex, no men, no women, no children! Then there's Georges Perec's 285-page, ill-at-*e*'s novel *A Void* (1978, in French and recently translated into English). But no writer has ever equaled the lipogrammatical achievement of Spanish writer Carlos Ibañez, who in each of his twenty-eight novels banished a single and different letter of the Spanish alphabet.

XI. A Letter-Perfect Sideshow

I could have added to the "X files" *"ch:* Arantxia," from the first name of Spanish tennis star Arantxia Sanchez Vicario, but the example is not sufficiently English.

I vacillated about whether to include golfer Justin Leonard among the *aeiou* names, fearing that he was not sufficiently famous. But the man made the decision for me when he went out and won the 1997 British Open at the age of twenty-five and then placed second in the 1997 PGA Championship.

The various examples of five contiguous vowels are surpassed by the name Potooooooooo, assigned a British racehorse born in 1773. That name was pronounced "Potatoes" (Pot + eight *o*'s).

WASHERAYETAGEMUD isn't a word, but it is a letter chain in which each group of three consecutive letters — *was, ash, she, her, era, ray, yet, eta, tag, age, gem, emu, mud* — forms a word with no word repeated. An analogous chain of four-letter words is linked through TSARIDESK.

Sources

The most valuable source-ry for this book has been *Word Ways: The Journal of Recreational Linguistics* (hereafter listed as *WW*).

Because anagrams and palindromes have become part of our folklore, they exist in various forms and with various attributions, making it difficult to identify their original authors. Here all anagrams and palindromes are listed alphabetically with their earliest known sources. The anagrams are cited by phrase, the palindromes by key first and last words.

I. The Bandwagon

Bilingual grammagram word grid submitted by Woody Rowe.

Al Gregory provided a number of the homophones and homophonic categories.

Thanks to Pocket Books for permission to adapt the following poems from two of my books:

"A Bazaar Tail," *The Miracle of Language* (1991), pages 42-43; "A Heteronymble Poem," *Crazy English* (1989), page 80; "A Hymn to Heteronyms," *Crazy English,* pages 82, 84.

"An Apostrophe to Love," Dave Morice, *WW,* November 1987.

II. Ana Gram the Juggler

Of great value in constructing the Ana Gram narrative were Peter Newby's *Pears Advanced Word-Puzzler's Dictionary* (Pelham Books, 1987) and *Word Ways' The New Anagrammasia* (1991).

ACT ON A BAR, Hoho. A-I, APT, PROPER, Nypho. AH, AN ART GEM!, Guidon. AM IN UNITY, Balmar. AMEN STORIES, Lord Baltimore. AN AIR MESS, Hoho. AN ELEGANT MAN, Nympho. ARCH SAINT, Viking. *ARS MAGNA,* DCVer.

BUTCHER THY HATE, Remardo. BLAND SPIELER, AwlWrong.

CARE IS NOTED, DCVer. CLOBBER US, MAN, Talon. COME TRUST UP HERE, Enavlicm. CONVERSATION, Sam Weller. COURT POSERS, Jason.

DEMON ALE, Plantina. A DIRE PATH, Kamel. DIRTY ROOM, T.H. DUE RESPECT, Longman.

ENTAILS SINS, Sphinx. ENTER, ASP, Vulcan. AN EVIL SOUL'S SIN, Donatello. EXITS ON CUE, Steven Marlboro.

FELONS CRY, "NO MATE IN IT," DCVer.

GOLDEN LAND, *Farmer's Almanac,* 1812. GRAND OLD EVILS, Johank. A GRIM ERA, Nox.

HAS TO PILFER, EssEll. HE IS IN A NET SPORT, AbStruse. HE UNCIVIL AT A MS., Rho. HELP OUT MY NEED, David Shulman. HE'S LETTER POST MANAGER, Tunste. HE'S LEFT IT, DEAD: R. I. P., SittDowne. HOT SUN, OR LIFE IN A CAR, Josefa Heifetz (to which we append Heifetz's THE SAN FRANCISCO BAY AREA/CHANCE STAY, OR SAFE IN A BAR).

I A USSR, Yerces. I AM AN ARTIST, AND I BLESS THIS IN ME, Dave Morice. I CALL A MISCOUNT, Jason. I DUB IT A MIRACLE!, Tunste. I NAME NOT, Spud. I NO RASCAL, PAL, EmmoW. I PLAY ALL THE ABC, XSpected. I, RICH METER, AID IN THY SONG, Evervic. ILL FED, Enavlicm. I'M A DOT IN PLACE, AChem. I'M A HACKER, SON, Atlantic. IN A DISTEMPER, Viking. IS A LANE, AwlWrong. IS FINANCE LURE, BigDaddy. IS INANE, Hoodwink. IS NO AMITY, Lord Baltimore. IS PROPERTY, Arty Fishel. IT HEARS, Lee Sallows. IT'S NO POT, ProfPampelm+.

JOYFUL FOURTH, KingCarnival.

LEAST IN SINS, NJineer. LITHE ACTS, MabelP. LOVE TO RUIN, Enavlicm.

MAD POLICY, Jemand. A MAIN GOAL: ME, Mangio. MAY END IT, Tut. MEN DAILY, Ulk. A MOB'S TOMB, Molemi. MOON STARERS, *Farmer's Almanac,* 1821. MUST RANT, DCVer. MYSTICS IN A HEAP, TH.

NAME FOR A SHIP, Mangie. NICE LOVE, SamSlick. NO SALOONS (HIC!) CALM YOU, Acorn. NO UNTIDY CLOTHES, Ellsworth. NO WIRE UNSENT, LeDare. NO MORE STARS, *Masquerade,* 1794. NON-FIRES, Osaple. NOT AGAINST, Barnyard. NOTED MISCALCULATIONS, Spica.

O, IS A BEST MECCA FOR YOUTH, Fred Domino. O, SHAME OF IT, Nightowl. OH, THERE'S SOME FUN, AChem. ON THE SLY, Longman. *ONCE + CUATRO,* Lee Sallows. ONE OLD FORT NOW, Lyrrad.

PEN MATE IN LOVE, Hoodwink. POETRY/TRY POE, Hoosier. PROBLEM IN CHINESE, Gemini.

REAL FUN, *Masquerade* magazine. RELAX, ENSURE COITUS, Dmitri Borgmann. A ROPE ENDS IT, AirRaid. A ROTTING INSIDE, Archimedes. RUN,

PEST!, Viking. RUNS A TREAT, WillieWildwater.

SEE? IT'S VIOLENT!, April'sChild. SHALL YET COME, MCS. SHE CHECKS CORN AT OTHER SIDE, Susan Thorpe. SLICK RIME, Hexagony. SOW IT, LAD, Remardo.

TENDER NAMES, Jo Mullins. THEY SEE, Anonyme. TIDIER ROOMS, Sally. *TRECE + DOS,* Lee Sallows. A TRUE SIGN, Nelsonian. TWELVE + ONE, Martin Gardner.

VIDEO SEX MART, TutOwl. VOICES RANT ON, SamWeller.

WARM, INDOLENT, Dmitri Borgmann

parental/paternal/prenatal, Borgmann, *Language on Vacation,* p. 107.

VIOLETS poem: Xavier Balilinkinoff, *WW,* February 1969.

The analysis of *star* was suggested by Al Gregory.

III. The Palindromedary

"Elba Fable": Dave Morice, *WW,* November 1987.

ADAM/ADA, John Lindon. A DOG!/PAGODA!, Lubin. AHEM!/HA! Stephen J. Chism. A/PAJAMA!, Joaquin and Maura Kuhn. A MAN APART/PANAMA, Kuhns. A MAN! A PLAN!/PANAMA!, Mercer. A NEW ORDER/ROWENA, Borgmann. ANNE/VIENNA, Leigh Mercer. ARE/ERA, Mercer. A SLUT/TULSA, Borgmann. AH, SATAN/NATASHA, Bergerson.

BARCLAY/CRAB, Mark Saltveit. BOSS/S.O.B, Chism. BUT/STUB, Linden. CIGAR?/TRAGIC, John Lindon

DEER/FREED, Mercer. DO NINE MEN/NOD, Borgmann. DID I DO/I DID, Howard Richler. DOG DOO/GOD, Chism. DRAW/COWARD, Bergerson. DRAW/UPWARD, Bergerson. DRAB AS A FOOL/BARD, Mercer. DUAL/LAUD, Salveit. DUDE/DUD, Jim Hebert.

DOC, NOTE, I DISSENT. A FAST NEVER PREVENTS A FATNESS. I DIET ON COD merits a special note. This masterpiece, which has been variously attributed to W. H. Auden, Penelope Gilliat, and others, was submitted by James Michie to a *New Statesman* contest in 1946 — and won only third prize! Michie told Howard Bergerson that he first heard it in 1945 from a mathematician, who hadn't personally written it either. The real author turns out to be Peter Hilton, British mathematician and codebreaker in World War II. One of Hilton's colleagues during the war remembers his pulling an all-nighter in 1943 and creating what many revere as the English-writing world's greatest long palindromic statement. DRAB/BARD, Mercer. DRAW/UPWARD, Mercer.

EGAD/BAD AGE, Borgmann. ELBA/AMIABLE, Kuhns. ELK CACKLE, John Connett. EMBARGO/GRAB ME, Borgmann. EMIL/LIME, Chism. EVE/SIEVE, Lindon. EVE, MAIDEN NAME/EVE, Lindon. EWE ERA/EWE, John Ashkenas.

GATEMAN SEES/NAME TAG, Mercer. GO HANG/HOG, John Agee. GOD! A RED NUGGET/DOG, Mercer. GOLF?/FLOG, Mercer.

HE/DOG, EH?, James Thurber.

I MAIM/MIAMI, Borgmann. I SAW DESSERTS/WAS I, Bergerson. I'M A MADAM/AM I?, Bergerson.

LAY A WALLABY/AL, Mercer. LID/DAFFODIL, John Pool.

MA IS/AS I AM, Mercer. MADAM, I'M ADAM, Mercer. MADAM IN EDEN, I'M ADAM, Borgmann. MARGE/ TELEGRAM, Bergerson. MIX A MAXIM, Chism.

NAMED UNDENOMINATIONALLY/NUDE, MAN!, Borgmann. NAMED UNDER A BAN/NUDE MAN, Lindon. NAOMI/I MOAN, Willard Espy. NEVER/EVEN, Espy. NIAGARA/AGAIN, Bergerson. NO/OPPOSITION, J. A. Campkin. NO TRACE/CARTON, Pool. NOW, NED/WON, Mercer. NURSE/RUN!, Mercer.

OH WHO/OH WHO?, E. J. McIlvaine.

PANDA/NAP, Pool. POOR/DROOP, Bergerson.

RATS GNASH/STAR, Mercer. RATS/STAR, Bergerson. RISE TO VOTE, /SIR, Bergerson.

SIDES/IS, Linden. SIR/IRIS, Borgmann. SIR/SAFARIS, Connett. SO MANY DYNAMOS, Pool. SIT/OTIS, Borgmann. SLANG/SIGNALS, Chism. STAR/DEMOCRATS, Kuhns. STELLA/WALLETS, Borgmann. STOP!/RUMPOTS, Mercer. STRAW/WARTS, Mercer.

TEN/NET, Mercer. TOO/HOOT, Morton Mitchell. TRAPEZE/PART, Kuhns. UNGASTROPERINITIS/GNU, Lindon.

WAS IT/ CAT I SAW?, Marvin Terban. WON'T/NOW?, Borgmann.

YO! BOTTOMS/BOY!, Bergerson

Word-unit palindromes: A. Ross Eckler, *WW*, November 1987; DID HANNAH/HANNAH DID, Peter Newby, *WW*, November 1995. FIRST LADIES/LADIES FIRST, Peter L. Stein, first prize in Will Shortz's contest on

Weekend Edition, NPR. SO PATIENT/SO, Lindon. YOU CAN CAGE/YOU?, Martin Gardner, *Scientific American,* August 1970.

Particularly Adroit Language Image Nicely Duplicating Reversed-Order Message Exactly, Robert L. Patton, Jr., *WW,* February 1973.

IV. Big-Name Acts

DAD, EVEN A MA, Spreggs. DARE A LEWD CYNIC, Andy Aaron. DARE SHUN ISLAM, O.V. Michaelsen. FLIT ON, CHEERING ANGEL!, Lewis Carroll. GENERAL TAXED EARTH, Bergerson. GENUINE CLASS, Dick Cavett. GREATEST BORN IDEALIST, Bolis. HE'LL DO IN MELLOW VERSE, Ahmed. IS AS QUEENLY ON DECK IN JEANS, Marjorie Friedman. LAST SCOT WRITER, Hercules. PERSON WHOM ALL READ, Verdant Green. RADIUM CAME, S. James Nesi. ROLE: TO SERVE ALONE, Friedman. TEAR IT MAN. I ATONE, Modern Sphinx. WON HALF THE NEW WORLD'S GLORY, Walsh.

Presidential anagrams: If not otherwise noted, A. Ross Eckler, *WW,* February 1977.

A WORD WITH ALL: I'M FAT, Sphinx. ELEANOR, KIN, LAST FOND LOVER, Mary Hazard. LOVE? A COLD ICING, David Williams. HE DID VIEW THE WAR DOINGS, Mary Hazard. LOVED HORSE; TREE, TOO, Hazard. NIX HUSH CRIMINAL ODOR, Mike Morton. NO NINNY, HE'S ON JOB LADS, Borgmann. RASH ARMY RUNT, Hazard. REAL WINNER? HIM A LAGGARD, Jo Mullins. INSANE ANGLO WARLORD, Mike Morton.

The mass sinning palindrome is built on the foundation of a sentence in Dmitri Borgmann's *Language on Vacation,* p. 65.

Many of the famous-name palindromes were cobbled by the winners of a March 1992 *Games* magazine competition, reported in *WW,* May 1992. See also Dave Morice, *WW,* November 1991.

Additional sources include: CAIN: A MONOMANIAC, Andrea E, Cantrell. EH? DID ZORRO/DID HE?, Chism. DRAT SADAM, A MAD DASTARD, attributed to Clement Wood and others. HE'S A CARAMEL/EH?, Saltveit. LIAM/MAIL, Gregory. MAD ZEUS/SUEZ DAM, Espy. MAN, NO HAM/MCMAHON, Mercer. NO/MADISON, Morice. NO X/NIXON, Martin Gardner. NOW RELY/WON, Morice. O NOTE/VETO, NO!, Morice. RAW?/TRAMP AT WAR, Morice. ROB/GABOR, Espy. SAD, I'M MIDAS, Chism. SIS, IS/ ISIS?, Chism. SAD/MIDAS,

Tony Augarde. SUMS/ERASMUS, Borgmann. TARZAN/RAT, Irvine. TO LAST/A LOT, attributed to Edward Scher and others. WANT/ NAW, Borgmann.

T. ELIOT/TOILET, Alastair Reid.

Most of the palindromic brand names were captured by Robert Funt in *WW,* November 1981.

Most of the semordnilapic brand names were identifed by Dave Silverman and Howard Port in *WW,* May 1975, and Borgmann in *WW,* August 1975.

V. Clown Cars
A number of the non-meaningful charade words appear in various lists compiled by Steve and Sheila Toth. See *WW,* May 1996.

supermathematical: Dmitri Borgmann, *Language on Vacation,* page 111.

A BAR, ETC., Harry Ober.

CARS KILL/CAR SKILL, Andrew Belsey

MEND A CITY, Doug Frank

SO, A POP ERA, Michael-Sean Lazarchuk.

NOT ABLE/NO TABLE, Bennet Cerf

TO READ OR, SIGN IF I CAN'T; AM I ABLE TO GET HER?, Dmitri Borgmann, *Language on Vacation,* p. 111.

HATH OUTRAGE/LOOM!, Robert Funt, *WW,* February 1991; FLAMING, OPALESCENT/HARK!, Bergerson.

Reverse snowball words, Boris Randolph and Ralph G. Beaman, *WW,* May 1978.

The bookend words were discovered by Tom Pulliam, *WW,* November 1979.

Missy Clinebell and Barbie Henderson, two seniors at Tremont (Ill.) High School, found the hidden *Will I Am.*

VI. The Shrinking Spotlight
Pearl/pear/pea, Dave Morice.

HOW HIS OLD RUSSIAN HAT/EARS, Borgmann, *Language on Vacation,* p. 114.

A number of the curtailments appear in Ralph G. Beaman's disquisition,

WW, February 1976.

A number of the beheadments appear in *WW,* May 1990.

VII. Kangaroo Words

Of significant value to the gathering of the exhibits in "Kangaroo Words," "Words on a Wire," and "A Letter-Perfect Sideshow" was Chris Cole's "Word Records from Webster's Third," *WW,* May 1990.

VIII. The Acro Bat

Iraq/Iran and *Ireland/Iceland,* Al Gregory.

The shiftwords appear in Leonard J. Gordon, "Letter-Shift Words in the OSPD," *WW,* February 1990.

Oui/yes, A Ross Eckler. *Abjurer* +13 = *nowhere; primero* + 3 = *sulphur,* Dmitri Borgmann.

Phallus/Alice Faye, Doug Heller; *trash/ashtray,* Will Shortz.

"True But Outré," Dave Morice, *WW,* August 1995.

"Ill Wit," K. F. Ross, *Mensa Bulletin,* April 1969.

IX. Words On a Wire

Mr. Jock, TV quiz Ph.D., bags few linx is generally attributed to Clement Wood.

"Echo," adapted from Dave Morice, *WW,* November 1997.

AHTAWAIH, by Dave Morice, *WW,* May 1996.

Post office abbreviations, Bruce Pyne, *WW,* August 1986.

Lacerated, Borgmann, *Language on Vacation,* page 111.

Six-letter and seven-letter anchored palindromes: Leslie E. Card and A. Ross Eckler in *WW,* February 1974 and November 1986.

XI. A Letter-Perfect Sideshow

Jihad/hadji, Al Gregory.

X pronunciations: Dmitri Borgmann, *WW,* November 1984.

Gary Shandling/Gary's handling, etc., Dave Morice, *WW,* August 1994.

Whip Van Wrinkle, Don Hauptman, *Acronymania.*

TWENTY-NINE, Howard Bergerson.

Mine, Maxey Brooke, *WW,* May 1991
Smithery, Peter Newby, *WW,* February 1989
Tarmac/car mat, Simone van Egeren.
Pinking/kingpin, Dave Morice
The silent hosts are developed from a list by Dmitri Borgmann.

XII. *The Midway*
Australia/Austria, Al Matthews.
"When Sandy sees a flying crow," Dave Morice, *WW,* November 1991.

Re-Sources and Re-Creations

So you're still here? Then you must be a psychically mobile logolept who enjoys the Collide-O-Scope of Letter Configurations. Even though we've folded our tent, we'll offer you a single shelf of recreational word books so that the alphabet can continue to leap and pirouette for you:

Augarde, Tony. *The Oxford Guide to Word Games.* Oxford: Oxford University Press, 1984.

Bergerson, Howard W. *Palindromes and Anagrams.* New York: Dover Publications, 1973.

Bombaugh, C. C. *Oddities and Curiosities of Words and Literature.* New York: Dover Publications, 1961 (originally published in 1890).

Borgmann, Dmitri A. *Language on Vacation.* New York: Charles Scribner's Sons, 1965.

Brandreth, Gyles. *The Joy of Lex.* New York: William Morrow and Company, 1980.

_____. *More Joy of Lex.* New York: William Morrow and Company, 1982.

Donner, Michael. *I Love Me, Vol. I.* Chapel Hill, N.C.: Algonquin Books, 1996.

Eckler, Ross. *Making the Alphabet Dance.* New York: St. Martin's Press, 1996.

_____, ed. *Word Ways: The Journal of Recreational Linguistics.* Spring Valley Road, Morristown, NJ 07960; four issues a year, 1968–.

Espy, Willard R. *An Almanac of Words at Play.* New York: Clarkson N. Potter, 1975.

_____. *Another Almanac of Words at Play.* New York: Clarkson N. Potter, 1980.

_____. *The Game of Words.* New York: Bramhall House, 1971.

Evans, Rod L., and Irwin M. Berent. *Getting Your Words' Worth.* New York: Warner Books, 1993.

Hauptman, Don. *Cruel and Unusual Puns.* New York: Dell, 1991.

Hellweg, Paul. *The Insomniac's Dictionary.* New York: Ivy Books, 1986.

Lederer, Richard. *Crazy English.* New York: Pocket Books, 1998.

Michaelsen, O. V. *Words at Play.* New York: Sterling Publishing Co., 1997.

Morice, Dave. *Alphabet Avenue.* Chicago: Chicago Review Press, 1997.

Index of Terms

About the Author

Richard Lederer is one of the premier writers about the English language, in all of its punny and scrambled glories. He has always been captivated by words. As a pre-medical student at Haverford College, he found himself reading the chemistry books for their literary value. As a student at Harvard Law School, he preferred studying the cases characterized by stylistic skill. Deciding not to waste his linguistic sweetness on the desert air, he became an English teacher at St. Paul's School in Concord, New Hampshire, and received a Ph.D. from the University of New Hampshire in English and linguistics. Dr. Lederer has since shared his heels-over-head fascination with language in such books as *Anguished English, Crazy English,* and *The Miracle of Language.* He is a co-host of "A Way With Words" on San Diego Public Radio and is a regular contributor to *Writer's Digest* and the *Farmer's Almanac.* Richard Lederer invites you to explore his Verbivore's Web site at http://www.pobox.com/~verbivore and to e-mail him at richard.lederer@pobox.com.

About the Illustrator

In addition to being the illustrator for this book, **Dave Morice** is a noted wordsmith in his own right. For that reason, Richard Lederer often refers to Dave and to his logological findings inside the Circus. He received an M.F.A. from the Iowa Writers' Workshop in 1972 and taught children's literature at the University of Iowa for seven years. He has written more than twenty books, including *Poetry Comics: A Cartooniverse of Poems* and the children's book *A Visit from St. Alphabet.* His poetic creations can defy the boundaries of a book, or even the horizon: he has participated in 52 poetry marathons and crafted 1,000 poems at one sitting, a ten-hour blindfolded poem, a mile-long poem, a poem across the Delaware River, and one wrapping around a city block. Dave Morice lives in Iowa City, Iowa.